Bernadette Vallely is a life-long campaigner. She was born in London in 1961 and while still at school, became involved with the Anti-Nazi League, the Campaign for Nuclear Disarmament and later worked for the Anti-Apartheid Movement. The beginning of her commitment to environmental issues started when she worked with Friends of the Earth. It resulted in her setting up and becoming Director of the Women's Environmental Network.

She is author of *Fundraising is Fun: A Guide for Local Groups* and co-author of *The Sanitary Protection Scandal* which provoked public outcry and caused companies to stop the chlorine bleaching of nappies and sanitary towels.

Debbie Silver was born in London in 1960. She studied at Cambridge and at Essex Universities, and then worked at the Man in the Moon Theatre in London. While there, she adapted and co-directed Angela Carter's 'Puss in Boots' and 'The Lady of the House of Love'. Subsequently she worked in public relations and in publishing, and trained as a tutor for children with learning difficulties. In her spare time she writes and translates poetry, some of which has been published in *Cosmopolitan*. Her interest in the environment began about a year ago, and this is her first book. For her, as it will be for many of its readers, it is a beginning.

THE
YOUNG PERSON'S
GUIDE TO SAVING
THE PLANET

*Debbie Silver
and Bernadette Vallely*

With illustrations by
Christine Roche

VIRAGO

Published by VIRAGO PRESS Limited 1990
20–23 Mandela Street,
Camden Town,
London NW1 OHQ

A CIP Catalogue record for this book is available from the British Library

Typeset by CentraCet, Cambridge
Printed on recycled paper by
Cox and Wyman Ltd, Reading, Berks

To the only people who can get us out of this mess

Acknowledgements

When you write a book like this you get information from all kinds of sources. First we want to thank all the organisations who sent us their information and research.

We also want to thank Ann Link and Isobel, Alison Costello, Anne, Charo and everyone at The Women's Environmental Network; Julie Brown and John Adams at Friends of the Earth; Sue Adams at Greenpeace, Anne Chauveau; Judith Silver; Lennie Goodings and all at Virago. Very special thanks go to Colin Mulberg for reading and commenting on the first draft, and to Stewart Boyle for his expert help and loving support.

20% of the authors' proceeds from this book go to The Women's Environmental Network. Virago is also donating a percentage of its profits from this book. WEN works internationally, building links with women who are trying to save the planet. We need supporters all over the world. Join us and help spread the message. Send £1.00 for an information pack and magazine to WEN, 287 City Road, London, ECIV ILA.

Contents

Change to Green

Glad you chose to take a look,
This isn't just another book,
Read it – you'll see what we mean,
We think you'll want to change to green!

Rub your eyes and look around,
Litter lying on the ground,
Bottles, cans and polythene –
Take the tip and change to green!

Forests going up in smoke,
Cities fit to make you choke,
Nowhere left to be that's clean –
Take a breath and change to green!

Animals and plants have died,
People starve to feed our pride,
For the life that might have been
Take a stand and change to green!

There's so much that isn't right,
It could get you *well* uptight,
So make a start and change the scene –
The lights are flashing – change to green!

Preface

You're reading this book because you care about the environment. You're right to care. The environment needs you as it has never done before. It must have your help to survive. Every day, we hear more about the disasters that face us on this planet. Animals and plants are dying, becoming extinct at the rate of one species every day. Seas and rivers are being filled with rubbish. The air is being poisoned with chemicals and smoke. And these are only a few examples of how the way we have lived until now has damaged our world.

But it's not all bad. Lifestyles are already beginning to change as people become aware of what is going on and make choices to live in a way that is less damaging to the planet. Group campaigns are saving seals, rainforests, countryside. Governments and world leaders claim they have the environment at the top of their lists. 'Green' is becoming a household word. It's an exciting time to be green and your help is crucial.

This book is about what you personally can do to save the planet. It is a handbook, a guide with suggestions for action. We hope that you will take up some of them and add more of your own.

Every single step you take towards being green will help save the planet. It is our home. It is worth saving.

Quiz: How green are you?

Here is a quiz to see how green you are and how well informed you are about the environment. Try it now, again when you've finished the book, and again in six months' time, when you have taken some action.

Green facts

Choose one answer for each question. Correct answers are at the end of this part of the quiz. Score one point for every answer you get right.

1. We should take the lead out of petrol because
a) it makes it cheaper
b) it causes acid rain
c) it damages children's brains

2. Switching off lights is good because
a) it saves money
b) it reduces radiation in the lower atmosphere
c) it helps prevent cataracts in the eyes

3. Using environmentally friendly washing powder will
a) preserve the fibres in your clothes
b) stop poisonous deposits building up in your washing machine
c) prevent overgrowth of river plants

4. Recycling means
a) buying second-hand things

b) putting waste back into service
c) making gas from landfill sites

5. E-numbers are
a) types of food additives
b) types of energy-saving products
c) products that are environmentally friendly

6. Cutting down on meat in your diet is a good idea because
a) it reduces the greenhouse effect
b) it could stop rainforests being cut down
c) it stops you eating so much saturated fat
d) all of the above

7. We are burning the rainforests at the rate of
a) an acre a day
b) an acre every hour
c) an acre every second

8. The number of unnamed animal species living on a rainforest tree can be as high as
a) 100
b) 1,000
c) 10,000

9. Organic farming is
a) farming without the use of machinery
b) growing food without chemicals
c) growing vegetables in your garden

10. Radiation can cause
a) leukaemia
b) bilharzia
c) Alzheimer's disease

11. CFCs are
a) damaging the ozone layer
b) increasing the greenhouse effect
c) both of the above

12. The Irish Sea is
a) the most radioactively polluted in the world
b) increasing the greenhouse effect
c) where most of the seals have died in the past few years

13. Tartrazine is
a) a kind of plastic, used for floor tiles and double-glazing
b) a travel-sickness drug
c) a food additive that causes hyperactivity in children

14. Acid rain causes
a) trees to die
b) skin cancer
c) overgrowth of plants on reservoirs

15. The greenhouse effect is
a) the use of fertilisers to make plants grow faster
b) the gradual warming of the earth
c) the name of a global agriculture plan

16. Dioxins are
a) by-products of the fast-food business
b) the atoms that attach themselves to oxygen to form ozone
c) by-products of paper bleaching.

Correct answers: 1c; 2a; 3c; 4b; 5a; 6d; 7c; 8b; 9b; 10a; 11c; 12a; 13c; 14a; 15b; 16c.

Green living

Score one point for every 'yes' answer.

1. Do you read the list of ingredients on the food you buy?

2. Do you ever buy from a health-food shop?

3. Can you cook a vegetarian meal? (a meal, not a snack!)

4. If you are vegetarian, score 2.

5. Do you know how to switch off the hot-water system in your home?

6. Are your paper tissues or sanitary products labelled chlorine-free?

7. Do you switch off lights if nobody needs them on?

8. Does your school/college/home use recycled paper?

9. If you have ever organised campaigns on environmental issues, score 5.

10. For short journeys, do you regularly walk if you can?

11. For long journeys, do you regularly use a bike or public transport?

12. If your family has a car, does it run on unleaded petrol?

13. If your family doesn't have a car, score 2.

14. Do you buy ozone-friendly aerosols?

15. If you don't buy aerosols at all, score 5.

16. Do you buy cruelty-free products? (those not tested on animals)

17. If you have ever written to a manufacturer to complain about their product, score 5.

18. Do you belong to an environmental pressure group?

19. Can you name one endangered species?

20. Do you know where your nearest bottle bank is?

21. Do you collect aluminium cans for recycling?

22. Do you collect newspapers for recycling?

23. Are you a non-smoker?

How did you score?

Add your scores from both sections to discover if you are:
> very pale green – scores under 10
> light green – scores 10–25
> mid-green – scores 26–42
> dark-green – scores 43–53.

VERY PALE GREEN or it wasn't my idea to do this quiz . . .

Scores under 10

There is a whole green world awaiting you. Read on, read on, read on!

LIGHT GREEN or maybe I don't feel so good about my can of deodorant . . .

Scores between 10 and 25

If you are light green you've already begun to notice that some parts of your lifestyle aren't very environment friendly. You make sure your aerosols don't contain CFCs, but you've never considered organic food. You think about eating less meat and your family sometimes buys free-range eggs. You wouldn't think twice about throwing away paper, cans and bottles but if someone gave you a nice set of recycled paper for your birthday, you'd be really pleased. You're a bit curious about all the fuss over environment problems and definitely want to find out more, as long as it isn't too difficult. You'd like the shops to stock a good range of things to choose from and as long as the price is similar to your old brand, you'd probably buy an environmentally friendly product.

You realise that it is a good move to be green and you should definitely read on, and go greener.

MID-GREEN or what comes after the ozone layer?

Scores between 26 and 42

If you are mid-green you are really thinking about the way the planet operates and you know that everything you do – good or bad – will rebound on us sooner or later. You have made some changes to your lifestyle already. You always try to buy cruelty-free cosmetics or toiletries and you never buy aerosols. You probably insisted that your family's car run on lead-free petrol and you want them to buy environmentally friendly washing-up liquid. You know at least one drastic statistic about the planet and you feel strongly about one endangered species. You eat chicken and fish but have almost stopped eating red meat. You eat fast food but sometimes wonder what's in it. You often watch environment programmes on television. You may have picked up a leaflet about an environmental or animal-rights group and you are thinking about joining.

Now is the time to take the leap and become an active green. Join a group, have fun and make an impact!

DARK GREEN or I put the planet first

Scores between 43 and 53

If you are dark green you take environmental issues very seriously and try to live in a way that doesn't damage our planet. You are probably a vegetarian or vegan and you've certainly tasted organic food. You use recycled paper but are constantly frustrated with the lack of recycling facilities in your area. You might be a member of an environmental organisation and you've probably started petitions to protest against a company's abuse of the environment. You have written letters to organisations and maybe even the government. Your friends think you are a bit obsessive but you've noticed that recently they have been coming around to your way of thinking!

At times you feel completely enraged and overwhelmed by the enormity of it all. Take a break, talk to like-minded friends and have some fun. Be cheered by the fact that people are becoming more aware and there will be changes.

What you do does count!

Introduction

What green really means

The word 'green' means different things to different people. Politicians, environmentalists and the general public will all have their own definition. Ours is based on four principles.

Conservation

Part of being green is preserving things and saving them. Conservation means keeping the world in a state where it is fit for us and the generations after us to live in. By looking after and preserving tropical forests we can stop animals, plants and birds from becoming extinct, and save the culture and lives of the tribal people who live there. By recycling we cut down on our needs and save resources. Every time you reuse a plastic bag you are putting conservation into practice.

Finding alternatives

Finding alternatives means trying to supply our needs in a way that is less damaging to the planet. It is a bit like conservation in that the priority is to look after things and 'put back what we take out'.

You can substitute fruit for sweets, bicycles for cars, recycled paper for ordinary paper or ecologically friendly washing-up liquid for the old kind. There are many other examples. You can get quite creative about finding safer substitutes.

The principle of finding alternatives operates in a wider sense as well. There are many substitution projects going on at the moment. Solar power, energy from the sun which won't run out, can be used to heat houses instead of energy from coal or oil. Food can be grown with fewer fertilisers, which means that the soil will be healthier.

Choosing

Everything has a price. The way you spend your time and money is very important; it can affect the welfare of the planet. If you spend your money on goods that will last and that you can use again and again, you will be doing more to help the planet than if you buy things you can only use once and then throw away. If you spend your time reading labels, being active and campaigning or even just thinking twice before you buy, you will be using your own resources – your money and time – in a way that helps to put your principles into practice. The more people who put their money and time behind things that don't damage the planet, the more the green message will spread.

Choosing means being aware of the power you have as a consumer and what you can do. Throughout this book, we have assumed that you have some spending power and that you will have more as time goes on. We also know that some environmentally friendly goods are expensive.

Caring

Caring means having respect for everything that shares our planet with us. It means looking after plants and animals as well as other human beings and trying to make sure that our lives don't damage theirs. It means looking after our own health, too. It means trying to make sure that food, energy and other resources are distributed fairly, so that everybody gets what they need. It means looking after ourselves and our planet.

Everything that we do is interconnected. Every breath we take on this planet makes us part of the complex, living, breathing entity that is the world. Every act has a consequence. What we do today can rebound later, even if we are not around to see what happens. Caring means recognising this and doing everything we can to make sure that we are not hurting other people and the world by the way we live.

Putting these principles into practice means taking some kind of action.

Action

Whether you're a light green, a mid-green or a dark green, there are going to be things you can do to help save the planet. This section tells you more about how to take action.

Action means different things to different people. One person might stop buying a particular product. Another might think twice about buying toiletries that are tested on animals. Another might start a discussion group at school or college. Another might choose one particular subject and work on a project or campaign, such as helping save a local wood or pond from developers. You can take action on your own or with a group. By taking action, you will be making it clear to people what you think and what you believe – and you will be helping the planet too.

Personal action

The starting point is personal action, which is about changing your own habits. You can make a personal choice about the sort of food you eat, the products you buy and the books and newspapers you read. By being aware of what is happening in the world, by reading or watching the news, you can decide for yourself where you want to start helping to save the planet. Here are some examples of personal action:

You can learn to ride a bike.

You can learn to cook, so *you* can decide what you want to eat.

You can find out more about what is in the products you buy, by reading food labels and lists of ingredients.

You can build a pond or grow a wild-flower garden, creating places where insects and birds can live.

You can ask questions. Why is nuclear power considered by some people to be dangerous? Why do some companies still use animals for testing? Why are seals dying? In finding out the answers to these questions, you will be able to decide what you want to do to change the situation.

Throughout the book, you will find many more suggestions for what you can do as an individual. Some ideas may appeal more to you than others. Perhaps you'd much rather build a pond than bother about reading labels. Begin with what you enjoy. You can't do everything at once. But everything you do will make a difference. For more ideas, see 'More things to do', below.

Group action

If you think all this sounds a bit like 'it's me against the world', then you're wrong. There are millions of people all over the world who are members of environmental groups. There are many more who might want to join one.

There are local, national and international organisations. You may want to be part of a national structure, like Friends of the Earth's Earth Action.

Or you may want to start a group of your own with your friends. At the end of the book is a checklist for setting up and running your own group. Whether it is a discussion group, a group to make sure that your school is litter-free or a group that raises funds for environmental causes, there is a lot you can do.

Under many of the sections in the book we give names of groups who are campaigning on particular issues. If you want to join them, look up the addresses in the back of the book.

More things to do

These are things that you can do either on your own or in a group.

Information

The environment is a really big issue these days, and once you start looking, you'll find information on it all around you. Why not start regularly reading a newspaper? Or watch out for programmes on TV and the radio. You'll be likely to find at least one story on the environment. Check your library or your bookshop for books on environmental topics. The more information you have, the more you can spread the green message around.

Projects

It is quite likely that at some stage of your educational career you will have to do a project. Why not do one on an environmental issue or on the environment in general? This will not only make you better informed, it will also educate your teachers, your examiners and even your family. Finding out facts for a project is a great way to make contact with people who are working for the environment.

Writing letters

Letters can be very influential. There is something very powerful about people putting pen to paper to state something they care about. Letters do get read, and sometimes even get published in newspapers and magazines. Politicians take note of the size of their mail bag on any particular issue.

You can write a letter on your own, or a joint letter with a group of friends or your family.

First find out whom to write your letter to. If you are writing to a manufacturer, their address should be on the product itself. Write first to the Customer Services Manager.

You don't have to be rude – you are more likely to get an answer if your letter is polite and well argued. Try to back up what you are saying with facts. See the sample letter on p. 110.

Keep a copy of your letter. Then, if you do not get a reply, you will be able to follow it up.

Remember that animals, birds and most living things on this planet don't have a say, but you do. So put pen to paper and make your voice heard!

Boycotting products

If you find out, from this book or just by asking questions, that you don't agree with the way that a particular product is made or sold, you can boycott it – that is, just stop buying it. A lot of people are already doing this. Boycotting a product gives a clear sign to manufacturers that something is wrong. You can make your point even clearer by writing a letter to them (see above).

How to use this book

Saving the planet is a tall order. The environment comprises everything around us. Start with what interests *you*. Here are some guidelines.

The book contains short entries for the major environmental issues we can do something about, arranged in alphabetical order. If you already know that some subjects interest you more than others, turn to them first. Within each entry, you may very well find some words in CAPITAL LETTERS. This means that you can look up that word or term for more information.

Say, for example, that you want to find out about RECYCLING. If you look up the entry, you will find BOTTLES, CANS, PAPER, WASTE and LANDFILL SITES appear in capitals in the text. All these sections will give you further information about recycling, so we suggest you read them too.

But what if you don't know what interests you yet? We suggest that you just open the book at random and start reading.

At the end of every entry you will find a list of suggestions under the heading *What can you do?* These are arranged in order ranging from 'light green' to 'dark green'. Try following the earlier suggestions first. If you're already doing what they recommend – great!

The back of the book contains two lists: addresses of groups and books for further reading. You will find the addresses of every organisation we quote in the *What can you do?* sections as well as addresses of other organisations worldwide. The list of books contains those we ourselves have found useful, and we hope you will read them, for project work or just for interest.

In this book we have used the term 'developed' to describe countries that are mostly industrial and fairly well-off, like Britain, West Germany, North America and Australia. We have used the term 'developing' to describe poorer countries, mainly in the South, like Africa, India, the Philippines and South America. We do not necessarily agree with these terms but we are using them to describe the economic position of these countries at the present time.

Acid rain

Acid rain doesn't burn us, and it has got nothing to do with drugs, but it has a burning effect on trees and buildings. It is a result of AIR POLLUTION. Our factories, our CARS and our power stations belch out hundreds of tonnes of polluting substances every day. One of the environmental problems created by these substances is acid rain.

Acid rain is created when gases like sulphur dioxide, nitric oxide and nitrogen dioxide rise up into the atmosphere from smoke and exhaust fumes. There, they mix with water to form dilute acid. This acid falls down to earth again as rain or snow. Black snow, as acid as vinegar, fell in Scotland in 1984.

Acid rain affects everything it falls on. Rivers, lakes and forests are at risk throughout Europe and North America. In Sweden, more than 18,000 lakes have become acidic, 4,000 of them very seriously indeed. This kills fish and drives out fish-eating wildlife.

FORESTS are particularly badly affected by acid rain, and in many places previously green, luxuriant trees show bare branches at the top, stripped of foliage. In West Germany, 50 per cent of trees are affected and, unless some curb is placed on pollution, the figure is certain to rise. In Austria, if nothing is done, scientists and environmentalists have predicted that there will be no trees left at all by 1997.

Buildings 'die' too. Some of the most beautiful historic buildings in the world are being eaten away by the dilute acid rained on them. Nôtre Dame, Cologne Cathedral, the Taj Mahal and St Paul's Cathedral have all been damaged.

Some countries, like Sweden, are trying to tackle the acid-rain problem by using safer technology to burn their coal, oil and gas. New power plants use a method called fluidised bed combustion, which cuts sulphur emission down by 80 per cent. In Wilmshaven, in Germany, sulphurous smoke is sprayed with lime to produce gypsum, which is then used for building roads. Developing technologies like this may raise the price of electricity a little, but will save millions of trees, plants and animals.

■ *What can you do?*

Turn out lights when you leave a room; switch off television sets and other appliances when they're not in use. Reduce your own energy consumption. This means power stations will be putting out less pollution (see ENERGY CONSERVATION).

If you can, don't use cars when you could safely walk, cycle or use PUBLIC TRANSPORT instead. This will help cut down on car exhaust emissions.

Join Friends of the Earth's acid rain campaign, and ask them where you can get a kit to test for acidification in your own area.

Additives

Food additives are found mostly in processed foods – biscuits, frozen dinners, dessert mixes and so on, which have been processed by a food manufacturer. Statistics say that the average British person consumes between 5 and 7 kg of artificial additives per year – the equivalent of over twenty aspirin-sized tablets of CHEMICAL additives *a day*.

Food additives can turn unappetising mushes of raw ingredients into 'cheese', 'chicken soup, 'tomato ketchup' and a multitude of other foods, by changing the food's natural colour and flavour. A packet of chicken soup or a fruit-flavoured dessert mix may not contain any chicken or fruit at all. Sometimes the soup and the dessert mix have exactly the same ingredients and differ only in the choice of synthetic colouring and flavouring.

Other additives include texture controllers, which make sure that food doesn't go lumpy or its ingredients separate while it is on the shelf, PRESERVATIVES, antioxidants, sweet-eners, mineral hydrocarbons and solvents.

Not all additives are bad for you. Some really are necessary, particularly the ones that preserve food. But many additives are superfluous.

Some food additives have been linked with asthma, eczema, rashes and watery eyes, as well as hyperactivity in children. Others, like the nitrites used to preserve meat, have been suggested as possible causes of cancer. Because additives, at least in Britain, are allowed to stay on the market until they are proven to be dangerous, we are eating a lot of untested substances. Food additives are a good example of how unnecessary CHEMICALS are working their way into our bodies every day.

■ *What can you do?*

Try to eat food which is fresh and cooked in your own home; then you know what is in it. ORGANIC food entirely avoids the use of chemicals, but the system of AGRICULTURE in the UK makes it expensive.

Look for healthy substitutes for processed food – fruit instead of sweets, nuts instead of crisps.

Find out how to read food labels (see E NUMBERS) and you can avoid the additives that are known to be dangerous.

See also ANIMAL TESTING (many food additives are tested on animals), FAST FOOD, HAMBURGERS.

Aerosols

We buy a staggering one million aerosols every day in Britain – to make us smell 'nice'; to make our hair stand on end; to make it flat; to spray walls. Some aerosols contain propellants that are environmentally damaging.

In 1988 two-thirds of our aerosols contained chlorofluoro-carbons – CFCS. These gases, used to propel the contents of the aerosol out in a fine spray, have been found to deplete the fragile OZONE LAYER which surrounds the earth. The ozone layer is our shield against the damaging effects of the sun's rays, and it is not only thinning but developing holes.

Many manufacturers have reacted to campaigns around the

3

world by moving away from using CFCs. Most aerosols are now filled with hydrocarbon propellants. These are less hazardous to the ozone layer but highly flammable if the cans are punctured or exposed to heat, and contribute indirectly to the GREENHOUSE EFFECT.

The synthetic chemicals that some products sold in aerosol form contain must also be questioned. For example, aluminium chlorohydrate (see DEODORANTS) is especially irritating to broken skin, and limonene, found in air fresheners, is a possible cause of cancer in animals. We spray these products in our homes or on our bodies, often near our eyes or on sensitive parts of the skin, without due care.

The disposal of aerosols is still an environmental problem. Aerosols are not BIODEGRADABLE and once we have thrown them away, they can still last for years in LANDFILL SITES and waste dumps, where they may explode and do more damage.

■ *What can you do?*

If you really must buy aerosols, make sure they contain no CFCs. They should carry a label marked 'ozone friendly' or 'environment/environmentally friendly'. Never spray them in your eyes or near a source of heat.

Dispose of them carefully, not in a place where direct sunlight could heat the gases they contain and make them explode. If you can't find a way to dispose safely of aerosols you have used, try sending them back to the manufacturer for disposal.

Try not to buy aerosols at all. Look instead for products in a different form, like roll-on deodorants instead of spray ones.

Agriculture

Agriculture is the use of land for growing things, usually food. The area of the world used for agriculture is about one and a half times the size of the United States. The methods of agriculture we use today are a problem for the environment because they are often destructive, even though they grow the food we need to survive.

Before the beginning of the century, farms used to produce a mixture of crops, and some of the land was used to raise animals, too. This gave the land time to rest between different crops. But now many farms produce only one crop. This is called the 'monoculture system'.

There are disadvantages to producing only one thing. The land becomes more easily exhausted because the same minerals from the SOIL are taken up by the crop year after year, and so those minerals have to be provided by chemical substitutes. A single crop is also more vulnerable to pests and weeds, so weedkillers and PESTICIDES have to be used to help it grow.

Crops used to be grown only on land that was suitable for them, but because the need for food is so great now, areas in the tropics are also being farmed (see RAINFORESTS). Chemicals have to be used in large quantities to help this unsuitable land produce the crop, which often does not end up in the mouths of the people who produce it (see GREEN REVOLUTION, MALNUTRITION). At the same time, the use of chemicals has meant that other areas of the world are producing too much. Milk lakes, butter mountains and grain mountains have literally built up in the European Community, where we destroy 76 kg of unwanted food *per second*.

The spread of agriculture is also harming the environment. Natural HABITATS are being destroyed. Soil is being overused and eroded. DESERTS are spreading. Chemical FERTILISERS are polluting soil and seas, and as a result the number of different species of plants and animals in the world is decreasing.

■ *What can you do?*

Consider becoming a VEGETARIAN. Several times more land has to be given over to agriculture to feed people on MEAT than on vegetable produce.

Ask your parents to consider buying ORGANIC food, which is healthier both for the land and for us.

Write to Friends of the Earth, the Soil Association and the Vegetarian Society, who have material on agriculture. Try to get your school, college or local library to mount an exhibition based on their information.

Spend a weekend growing food. Contact WWOOF (Working Weekends on Organic Farms).

Air Pollution

The air of our planet is being polluted by acid gases, dust, petrol and diesel fumes and poisonous CHEMICALS. These come from our CARS, our factories and our power stations.

ACID RAIN is seen by many as being the major air pollution disaster of our times, but there are other examples. One is the famous brown haze, or smog, which hangs over the Los Angeles basin in California. The chemical compounds in the smog are formed by the sunlight acting on gases in the air that come from vehicles, the burning of FOSSIL FUELS and various other industrial processes. They are poisonous, particularly to plants but also to humans. Melbourne, Ankara and Mexico City also suffer from this kind of smog.

Other cities have air-pollution problems of their own. In 1988 in Toronto, Canada, people were advised not to run or jog in the streets because they would breathe in too much polluted air if they did. In the summer of 1989, the British Lung Foundation suggested that Londoners should wear masks to protect them from the high levels of chemicals and pollutants in the city air. And cities in the developing world are beginning to suffer from industries that have been set up near them. Lagos, Jakarta and Calcutta are covered with a build-up of charcoal-caused smoke.

A major problem with air pollution is that it does not obey national boundaries. The planet's wind cycles and currents can carry pollution hundreds of miles away from its original source. So Britain is a large contributor to air pollution in Sweden and creates more for Norway than Norway does itself. The pollutants of the USA end up on the eastern coast of Canada.

Many countries in the world are trying to solve the problem of air pollution in various ways, either by trying to burn their FOSSIL FUELS more cleanly or by fitting catalytic converters to their CARS so fewer poisonous gases are produced. France even has a 'pollution brigade' who spot-check cars for what they are emitting – a bit like breathalysing car exhausts.

■ *What can you do?*

See the suggestions under ACID RAIN.

Consider wearing a mask if you have to walk or cycle for

long distances in a city. Contact the British Lung Foundation, who recommend that you should wear a mask if you are prone to lung problems like asthma or chest infections such as bronchitis.

Allergies

If you have ever had hay fever, you probably know how uncomfortable it is to suffer from an allergy. One in every five people is likely to suffer from some sort of allergy.

An allergy occurs when the human body becomes sensitive to a particular substance. The body's immune system thinks it is being attacked and produces more and more antibodies, which include powerful natural chemicals like histamine. These chemicals provoke physical reactions like asthma, eczema, watering eyes and runny nose. Allergic reactions can be so extreme that they result in death, though this is rare.

Some of the CHEMICALS in our environment could be triggering allergic reactions in our bodies. PESTICIDES, BEAUTY aids and food ADDITIVES are only some of the chemicals contributing to our bodies' daily dose of foreign substances.

The chemicals can also produce 'hidden allergy', where the body does not immediately react against a substance by rashes and hay-fever responses but instead gives way to long-term illnesses like depression and migraine.

Allergies are difficult to treat. Although symptoms of allergies can be relieved by medicine in the short term it cannot treat the cause. Only by eliminating chemicals from our bodies as much as possible will we be able to help cure allergies in the long run.

■ *What can you do?*

Try to become more informed about the artificial chemicals you are putting into your body, and see if you can avoid taking in quite so many.

If you think you may suffer from allergies, visit a doctor or homeopath, or try self-help by keeping a record of what you have been eating or been close to. You may discover the cause of your allergy yourself.

7

Read the shopping guide produced by Action Against Allergy.

Animal Testing

An estimated 400 animals are used *every hour of the day and night* in Britain for laboratory experiments. Mice, rats, guinea pigs, cats, dogs and other animals are used to test drugs, food ADDITIVES, BEAUTY products and household products. Animals are also used as models for psychological deprivation, stopped from sleeping or drinking water or separated from their mothers to see what effect this has on them. Pregnant animals are dosed to see if chemicals or drugs will affect their offspring. Live animals are given doses of poison gas and blown up in the interest of learning more about warfare.

The methods used for testing are usually painful to the animals. In the Draize eye test, the substance on trial is dripped into a rabbit's eye. The effects of the substance are observed for seven days. Ulceration, swelling, pus discharge and even blinding are common. In the LD50 test, a group of animals are force-fed a substance to see how much of it will kill the animals – the LD stands for 'lethal dose'. In skin tests, the animals' hair is removed so that the substance being tested can irritate their skin.

The animals' reactions to the drugs or CHEMICALS are tested by sampling their blood, dissecting them or observing their reactions. This includes noting how long it takes them to die from poisoning or experience pain, bleeding or discomfort.

Animals are also used for dissection in schools and colleges. Even though some schools, local education authorities and universities have found alternatives to live dissection – using computer simulations or films – some students still find that dissection is compulsory.

The usual argument for using animals for testing is that it is necessary because new substances can't be tested on humans. This is a difficult question to resolve, and you will find in this book that we quote the dangerous effects of certain chemicals on animals, not on humans. Animal testing is not always reliable, because many results of animal research simply do not apply to humans. Animals and humans are different species. Morphine, which is a depressant in humans, produces manic reactions in cats and mice; chloroform, which doesn't kill humans, kills dogs; penicillin kills guinea pigs and hamsters. Even though all drugs are tested on animals, there is no way of knowing absolutely what the results will be when the drugs are used on humans.

Animal testing is also slow and very expensive. Companies began in the 1980s to look at alternatives, and some of the major cosmetics manufacturers no longer use animals for testing. Shops like the Body Shop have helped dramatically to increase the availability of 'cruelty-free' cosmetics.

There are alternatives to using animals for research. Plant and animal cells can be grown in laboratory dishes containing a nutrient liquid, and used instead. Yellow fever and anti-viral drug research, polio research and cancer drug tests, which used a variety of animals, are increasingly being conducted in this way.

■ *What can you do?*

Choose not to buy make-up or toiletries that are animal-tested (look for a sign which says they haven't been, otherwise assume that they have).

Look into alternatives to pills for aches and pains, like plant-based homeopathic remedies.

If you find that you have to do dissections in science or biology lessons and want to opt out, write to the National Anti-Vivisection Society. They have a full list of suppliers of alternatives to dissection, including videos, computer simulations, films and models. The National Council for Civil Liberties has pledged to ensure that students have a right to refuse dissection without penalty.

Join one of the animal welfare and anti-vivisection (anti-animal testing) societies.

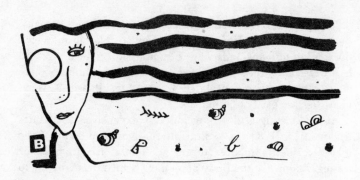

Batteries

When the battery runs out in your personal cassette, just as you are getting into the best group you've heard in ages – spare a thought for the power behind the music. The chemicals used in batteries are not good for us or for the environment. The European Community has asked manufacturers to remove some of the more dangerous chemicals they contain.

Many batteries are made from poisonous substances such as the HEAVY METALS cadmium, LEAD and mercury. Batteries also require a huge amount of energy in their manufacture: up to 50 times as much energy than they eventually provide for your radio or personal cassette player.

Rechargeable batteries are now available. They are made of cadmium and nickel, and they will last up to 50 times as long as a normal battery. They are a better environmental choice, although cadmium is extremely poisonous and we hope a safer substitute will soon be found.

■ *What can you do?*

Look for cadmium and mercury-free batteries, which can now be found in some supermarkets.

Buy and use rechargeable batteries.

Try to avoid buying equipment and presents that use batteries. Sometimes there are alternatives that use solar power.

Dispose of batteries with care. They are not BIODEGRADABLE and are dangerous if they leak. You can send them back to the manufacturer asking them to dispose of them safely.

Beauty

We care about the way we look. We want to look as good as possible. And there are a huge number of products that claim to be able to help us do so. Skin creams, make-up, hand and body lotions, nail polish, perfumes, bath oils, shower gels – toiletries of this kind are bought in millions throughout the world. Hundreds of millions are spent on advertising to encourage us to buy them. But some of these products can endanger our health and harm the environment.

Many toiletries contain CHEMICALS of various kinds, unless they say that they are made only from pure, natural products. Because we are putting so many different types of chemical on our bodies, we are lowering our resistance to them. For example, an estimated 40 per cent of the population could have ALLERGIES to petrochemicals, by-products of the oil and petrol industry used in make-up. If the origin of an ingredient is not listed on the label, we don't know what we are putting on ourselves. Petrochemicals are a source of water pollution too, and the factories who make the products may be polluting the environment in an effort to supply them to us. (See also DEODORANTS.)

Some toiletries are made directly from animal products. Lanolin, a common ingredient in skin creams, comes from the wool of sheep, and animal fats can be used in lipsticks.

Many toiletries are still tested on animals. Approximately 14,500 rats, rabbits and monkeys die every year in the UK from testing for make-up, skin creams and other products. (See ANIMAL TESTING.) But this is beginning to change. The first firm supplying 'cruelty-free' cosmetics and toiletries to become well known was the Body Shop, but other manufacturers soon joined in. In 1989, pressure from animal-rights groups and activists, as well as from people using their CONSUMER POWER to choose products that have not been animal-tested, made two of the largest beauty companies – Revlon and Avon – undertake not to use animals for testing any more.

We don't have to stop using toiletries or make-up. We can make a real difference to the way the beauty industry works by showing it what we will and won't buy. Beauty products are particular offenders in having a lot of unnecessary PACK-AGING, too. If we show that we want products made only with natural ingredients, which are not tested on animals, we can help the manufacturers get the green message.

■ *What can you do?*

Buy cruelty-free cosmetics and toiletries. Look for a label that says explicitly that the product hasn't been tested on animals.

Try to find natural alternatives to some of your toiletries. For example, instead of buying packaged perfume, you can mix your own personal blend by diluting natural essential oils from a health shop in a base oil like almond or jojoba. You can make good moisturising oils this way too – and lavender essential oil is great for getting rid of spots. So is witch-hazel lotion, which you can buy at the prescription desk of any chemist.

Try to buy from the smaller companies who are supplying natural beauty products which are not animal-tested. Your health shop is a good place to start. Companies include Beauty Without Cruelty, Cosmetics to Go (who supply by mail order) and Shahnaz, who make all-herbal products based on old Indian recipes.

Try to cut down gradually on the amount of toiletries you are buying and using. Do you really need a cupboard full of make-up when you don't use half of it regularly?

A useful book to have with you when you are buying is the pocket-sized *Cruelty-Free Shopper* from the Vegan Society. It contains a full listing of cosmetic products and toiletries that are not tested on animals and contain no animal products.

Support animal-rights organisations like Animal Aid and the RSPCA.

Biodegradable

The term 'biodegradable' is used to describe the way that substances break down in the environment. For example, a paper bag will break down over time into a collection of harmless substances like water, air and carbon. These substances can then be absorbed again into the natural soil, wind and water cycles of the planet.

It is a major problem that many of the products we use are 'non-biodegradable'. This means that they take an enormously long time – sometimes hundreds of years – to break down in the environment, and they can cause damage while they are still whole. The substances produced when, for example, FERTILISERS break down can be even more dangerous than the original fertilisers themselves.

PLASTIC can last for hundreds of years. Some shops and manufacturers are now labelling certain products, like plastic bags, as biodegradable, but unfortunately most are only 'biodestructable'. This means that the plastic breaks down in the environment to tiny particles that the human eye cannot see any more. The problem isn't necessarily solved – it's just put off. Truly biodegradable plastic is extremely expensive and even the British Plastics Federation doubt it can be used in every circumstance.

■ *What can you do?*

Cut down on the amount of DISPOSABLE goods you use.

Read the sections on PLASTICS and DIOXIN for examples of materials which take a long time to biodegrade and can be dangerous.

Try to buy products which will biodegrade easily. For example, paper that can be recycled rather than plastic products (see PACKAGING). Avoid AEROSOLS, which do not biodegrade.

Bottles

In Britain this year, about 6 billion glass bottles and jars will be bought – everything from cola, pickled onions and tomato ketchup to wine and marmalade. Five billion of these will go straight into the bin, and from there into LANDFILL SITES.

Glass can be either recycled or refilled. Glass from bottle banks, or from factory waste, can be melted down again to save energy and raw materials. A lot of energy can be saved – the equivalant of 136 litres of oil, which would be needed to make the glass from scratch, per tonne of used glass. In 1987 in Britain 32 million litres of oil were saved this way. Recycled glass also saved 1.2 tonnes of raw materials from every tonne used, and although the raw materials for glass (sand and other minerals) are plentiful, they still need to be dug out of the ground. So RECYCLING bottles preserves the countryside as well.

Britain is aiming for one bottle bank per 10,000 population by 1991. Other countries, like Switzerland and the Netherlands, have one bank per 2,000 head of population, and they are much more efficient recyclers as a result. In many parts of Canada and the United States, used bottles are collected separately in the same way as the rubbish.

Refilling glass is an even simpler process and is cheaper than the bottle-bank system, too. Milk bottles can be reused over and over – the average is 24 times. Glass jars can be used again in the home. As for other kinds of bottles – if the law required that all glass bottles carry a deposit which could be paid back to any customer who returned the bottles to the shop after use (returnable bottles), we would see more reused. West Germany uses this system very successfully.

■ *What can you do?*

Try not to throw any glass in the bin – use a bottle bank, which will also take glass jars you don't want to reuse for storage jars, vases, etc.

Don't throw away bottles that can be refilled, like milk bottles.

If your town or district does not have a bottle bank, write to the cleansing department of your local council (they will probably be based at the town hall). Ask for a bottle bank for your area, including your suggestions for where it should be sited.

Write to companies in your area who are heavy users of bottles and glass, like drinks manufacturers, or to the managers of supermarkets who sell a lot of glass containers. Ask them if they use glass recycling facilities, and if not, why not. Encourage them to set an example in being conscious of the environment.

Plastic bottles aren't as easy to recycle as glass. However, the Body Shop has a scheme where you can bring their empty containers back to be refilled. It's a good idea – and you get a 5 per cent discount.

Cans

If all the drinks cans (orange, cola, lemonade, beer and so on) used and disposed of in Britain in 1988 were placed end to end, they would have reached the moon: 4,450 million cans were thrown away. In energy terms, this is equivalent to throwing away half of every canful of oil.

Cans are made of either tinplate or aluminium, sometimes both in a mixture. Tin and aluminium are both expensive metals. The mining of them means that the environment is altered or even destroyed. There are instances of RAINFORESTS being cut down to mine bauxite, the raw material from which aluminium is made. Mining strips the soil and causes it to erode; it also pollutes water sources near the mine with the chemicals used to extract aluminium.

Most cans can be recycled (see RECYCLING). It makes environmental sense to recycle them – reusing scrap aluminium means a 95 per cent saving of energy. In the Netherlands, 43 per cent of tinplate packaging used by consumers is recovered every year, and in the USA, figures of over 50 per cent are being reached in recycling aluminium cans – over 30 billion cans per year. Sweden reclaims 95 per cent of theirs.

In 1989, Britain had about 190 Save-a-Can sites run by the Can Makers Federation, and scrap-metal merchants will take aluminium cans. Some will even pay. But as yet there is no centrally organised scheme for can recycling.

Mixed metals are of very little value to a scrap-metal dealer. The aluminium, steel and tin need to be separated, and one very simple step forward would be to label cans with the metal they are made of, as is done abroad. You can lobby for this. In the meantime, the only option is to sort your cans with a magnet (aluminium is non-magnetic).

■ *What can you do?*

Find out about can-recycling schemes near you. If the cleansing or refuse department of your local council can't help, write to the Can Makers Federation to see where your nearest skip is.

Take your own aluminium cans to your nearest Save-a-Can skip or to a scrap-metal merchant.

Join WATCH who, with the Aluminium Federation, are encouraging schools to collect aluminium cans.

Get in touch with Earth Action, the Friends of the Earth UK youth action group. Their action guide for the Waste and Packaging Day they held is full of further suggestions.

Cars

Many people see cars as a status symbol. XJ7's, sun-roofs, and faster fuel injection get people excited and exhilarated.

Cars are an accepted way of travelling for millions of people, and essential for some. Yet we underestimate the serious environmental problems they cause. Five thousand people die in accidents every year in the UK and many more are injured. AIR POLLUTION from car exhausts leads to illnesses like lung cancer, bronchitis and asthma. Congestion when too many cars cram on to the roads creates dangerous and dirty cities and town centres.

Cars run on petrol, which emits carbon monoxide, carbon dioxide, unburned hydrocarbons and oxides of nitrogen. These contribute to both ACID RAIN and the GREENHOUSE EFFECT. LEAD in petrol has been linked with damage to the central nervous system in adults and poor mental development in children. Its use was severely restricted in North America and some European countries several years before lead-free petrol was introduced in Britain.

Company cars, offered as a bonus to employees, encourage people to drive to work. Seventy-five per cent of all cars driving into London have some form of company assistance.

Parked cars encroach on space needed by cyclists and pedestrians.

Using cars encourages pollution, noise, fumes, illnesses and accidents, and the more roads that have been built, the more cars have filled them. Roads take up more space and money than our open spaces, and the Department of Transport has for decades favoured roads and motorways over cycle lanes, cycle paths and better, cheaper PUBLIC TRANSPORT.

It is time we started to reconsider our relationship with the car!

■ *What can you do?*

Walk, use public transport, or cycle (see CYCLING) more often.

Contact the Campaign for Lead Free Air (CLEAR) for information about lead in petrol.

Try doing a project on the transport in your area. Contact Transport 2000 for some really good transport-policy ideas.

Cash Crops

Cash crops are crops that are grown to sell to other countries. Over the past fifty years, large areas of land in the tropics and the developing world have been turned over to growing single crops like maize, soya, COTTON or sugarbeet. These crops are sold to the developed world to help the poorer countries meet their debts.

The land that is used for growing these crops is not necessarily suited to producing them on a large scale. The soil may be poor or the rainfall patterns may not provide sufficient water. This means that technology, in the form of machines, PESTICIDES and other chemicals, has to be brought in to help.

This kind of farming splits the community. Poor farmers cannot afford the technology to help the crop grow to fruition. Big agriculture companies take over and buy up the poor farmers' land. In tropical countries, the poor then go into the forests, where they cut and burn to make a living (see RAINFORESTS), while in other countries, like Mexico, people leave their homes and move to the cities to make a living. Many live in shanty towns, leaving their families behind and seeing them only rarely.

17

Women are particularly badly affected by the cash-crop system. Their traditional rights to land and place as farmers are lost to agricultural developments so they can no longer feed their families in their traditional ways. Their expertise and knowledge of seeds and soil are no longer valued.

Because the cash crops are sold to other countries (exported), it is difficult for the countries that grow them to feed their own populations. This leads to poverty and starvation (see MALNUTRITION).

■ *What can you do?*

Find out about the schemes run by international agencies like Oxfam, War on Want and Christian Aid which encourage people in developing countries to be self-sufficient.

Ask for information from the Intermediate Technology Development Group, who work to supply the technology that people in developing countries need rather than what it is thought they should have.

If you have a bank account, you can write and ask your bank what their loans to the developing world are for. You can also write to the minister for overseas development and the World Bank and find out the arguments in favour of the cash-crop system.

You might like to do a school project on how the price of cash crops is fixed.

Buying presents from Oxfam or Traidcraft supports co-operatives in developing countries.

See also AGRICULTURE, DDT.

CFCs (Chlorofluorocarbons)

Chloroflourocarbons (CFCs) are gases used in a wide variety of processs. They were invented in 1932 and are used because they are cheap, nonflammable, comparatively nontoxic and stable.

You probably have a CFC-containing product in your home. Any AEROSOL not marked 'ozone-friendly' or 'environmentally friendly' is likely to contain CFCs. Blown-foam packaging, such as that used in the trays that hold pre-packed meat and fruit in supermarkets, also often contains them. The rigid polystyrene containers that hold your FAST FOOD may contain them, although many fast-food manufacturers are aware of the problem and have made or promised to make changes. CFCs are also used in refrigerators, foam mattresses, car seats, fire extinguishers, some house-insulating foams, and for DRY-CLEANING.

CFCs are released into the air when a product containing them is destroyed. When CFCs reach the upper atmosphere, the CHLORINE they contain breaks down the fragile layer of ozone which surrounds and protects the earth (see OZONE LAYER). CFCs also retain heat, making them dangerous contributors to the GREENHOUSE EFFECT.

■ *What can you do?*

Avoid using AEROSOLS that don't carry a label stating they are CFC-free.

Avoid fast-food packaging if it does not say that it is CFC-free, and try to avoid those blown-foam trays used in supermarkets for meat and fruit. Instead, buy unpackaged food when you can.

The CFCs in old fridges need careful disposal. Your local council should be able to advise you on the best methods.

Support the ozone campaign run by Friends of the Earth.

Avoid solvents or chemical correcting fluids containing 1,1,1-trichloroethane which is an ozone destroyer.

Chemicals

Our bodies contain hundreds of different chemicals which act together to keep us alive. But our lifestyle today means that we are often taking in additional, artificial chemicals as well. About one million artificial chemicals are manufactured every year. It is difficult to test all of them thoroughly. Methods of ANIMAL TESTING often do not tell us all we need to know about them, and some of them may not even be tested at all. Chemicals may be present in the food we eat (see ADDITIVES, PRESERVATIVES) the air we breathe (see AIR POLLUTION), the products we put on our skins (see BEAUTY) and the water we drink (see DRINKING WATER). Our bodies do not always know what to do with them.

The human body has a sophisticated system for sorting out and storing good substances. Artificial chemicals confuse that system: they too are stored. So synthetic chemicals build up in our bodies, mostly in our fat. Some mothers' breast milk has been found to contain DIOXINS and DDT, which their bodies have held in the fatty breast tissue. These stored chemicals may harm us later in our lives. It is thought, for example, that our high artificial chemical intake and the high incidence of the cancers we suffer from are linked.

Because there are so many different chemicals around, we would do well to avoid them when we can. Many sections in this book deal with how to avoid taking in artificial chemicals unnecessarily.

■ *What can you do?*

Avoid using artificial chemicals whenever you can. Try buying ORGANIC food, avoiding clothes that need DRY-CLEANING and finding alternatives for BEAUTY and cleaning products.

Home Ecology, listed in the back of the book, has hundreds of ideas for cutting down on the chemicals we use every day.

Read the labels on what you buy. If a warning label says that a substance is unsafe for pets and children, it is logical to assume that it won't do you much good either.

Be careful how you dispose of chemicals.

If you want to find out more about specific chemicals, contact the London Hazards Centre. See also ALLERGIES, HAZARDOUS WASTE.

Chernobyl

In April 1986, an accident occurred at Chernobyl, a nuclear-power station Chernobyl in the Ukraine region of the Soviet Union. Radioactive emissions leaked from a huge fire in the central core of the power station. Although Chernobyl leaked only about 5 per cent of its total RADIATION, it took many weeks to stop the fires and shut the station down completely. Firefighters and other workers were exposed to large and dangerous amounts of radiation. Some died very soon after the accident; 32 deaths were officially recorded.

Hundreds of thousands of people who lived near the station

had to be evacuated and a radioactive cloud travelled thousands of miles across Europe contaminating crops, food, fresh meat and milk and water supplies. In some areas of Britain, sheep are still so radioactive that they are not fit for human consumption.

In the Ukraine, the area of Russia most directly affected, some women have been asked to sign a form saying they will agree not to have any children because of the increased risk of Leukaemia. Many people have died already from cancers, but it is feared that the authorities are trying to suppress this information. Extra cancer deaths from Chernobyl have been estimated at between 5,000 and 100,000. It may take between 5 and 40 years for cancers to emerge.

■ *What can you do?*

See our suggestions under NUCLEAR POWER.

Chipko

The Chipko movement began when women in northern India decided to campaign against their dwindling FORESTS being cut down. Women literally hugged the trees – *Chipko* means 'to hug' or 'to embrace' in Hindi – and refused to move away when the tree fellers arrived.

Some stories tell of women who were cut in half by foresters. In the area of Uttar Pradesh, the women's remarkable resistance and courage ensured that by 1980 a long-term ban was placed on commercial forest-cutting. This has saved a large area of forest.

The movement has spread throughout India and Chipko is now a strong campaigning group, planting trees and educating people about environmental issues.

The story of Chipko shows the power of simple, sustained action. It shows the success that can be achieved if enough people are convinced that what they do can really make a difference.

■ *What can you do?*

See if you yourself can campaign to plant or preserve the trees or forests in your area.

Read the section on GREEN PEOPLE to find out more about what groups of people are doing to protect their environment.

Hug a tree!

Chlorine

Chlorine is a greenish-yellow gas, highly irritating to the eyes, throat and lungs. Breathing it in large quantities can cause death – as it did when used in the First World War.

Chlorine is used in the chemical industry, and many of the compounds made with it are poisonous and persistent in the environment. It is also used to bleach wood pulp to make PAPER – a process that produces DIOXINS.

Many household bleaches contain the compound sodium hypochlorite. This may give off chlorine gas if mixed with other household cleaners or DETERGENTS.

Chlorine is also used to disinfect swimming-pool water. Some environmentalists are concerned that the chlorine joins with other substances in the water to make poisonous compounds, particularly if the water comes from peat moorlands or contains industrial discharges.

Drinking water is also lightly chlorinated.

■ *What can you do?*

Avoid chlorine where you can. A well-stocked health-food shop will be able to advise you on environmentally safe substitutes for household bleach. You can also find unbleached paper.

Try to find safely bleached or unbleached SANITARY PRODUCTS. These are beginning to appear on the market, and carry a label stating that they are chlorine-free.

Find out what your local swimming pool uses for disinfection. Some pools are now using ozone gas (this is not the same as the ozone layer!).

Consider using a water filter at home.

Cigarettes

The dangers of cigarette smoking to the smoker are well known and well documented. Smoking can cause lung cancer and is implicated in other cancers and heart disease.

Smoking is particularly dangerous for pregnant women because it affects the growth of children in the womb. Smokers' babies tend to be premature and underweight.

Smoking lowers the body's resistance to disease and has been found to trigger RADIATION-related cancers.

There are also environmental reasons for not smoking. Cigarette smoke is a pollutant, containing a variety of poisonous substances. Even if you yourself do not smoke you will be inhaling the equivalent of two cigarettes a week if you are surrounded by people who do. The poisons in cigarettes include DIOXINS, which are present in the tobacco and in the bleached white cigarette paper and are released when the cigarettes are smoked.

Tobacco is a CASH CROP. Although it is very difficult to trace a cigarette's exact origin, it is probably fair to assume that the tobacco in the cigarettes you or your friends smoke is grown in a developing country to help them meet their international debt. Land that could be used for crops to feed people may well be used instead to grow tobacco.

Tobacco is a costly crop to grow. It takes a lot of minerals out of the soil, and an estimated 12,000 sq km of forest per year is cut down to fuel tobacco-curing factories.

By not smoking you can safeguard the health of the planet as well as your own.

■ *What can you do?*

If you already smoke – a good percentage of teenagers, particularly teenage girls, do – try to give it up now. Smoking is a drug and it is very addictive: the longer you do it, the more difficult it is to give up (as one of the authors of this book has found!). Read books on giving up or join a group who are all trying to kick it.

Create 'smoke-free zones' at home or in the places you socialise – and stick to them.

Observe and publicise national and international non-smoking days.

Contact ASH (Action for Smoking and Health) for information.

Consumer Power

Consumer power means using the fact that you are a consumer – someone who buys and uses products – to exert pressure. Manufacturers and supermarkets are very conscious that they have to keep their customers happy.

You can use your consumer power in a number of ways. You begin by choosing. You can choose one particular item over another – for example, choosing to buy non-AEROSOL deodorants and antiperspirants instead of spray cans. You can go further by exerting pressure either negatively or positively.

Exerting negative pressure means boycotting, or *not* buying – for example, from manufacturers who test products on animals, who IRRADIATE food, who damage tropical RAIN-FORESTS, who use dangerous pesticides and chemicals or who have other bad practices.

Positive pressure means buying well. You can support companies who care about the environment by buying from them and spreading the word about their products to your family and friends.

Using consumer power is a way of taking action. We have already recommended it in our 'Action' section, and you will find it, in many forms, under a lot of the *What can you do?* headings. It has the advantage of being something that almost anyone can do, yet it does influence manufacturers and even other consumers to think about what really is in a product.

■ *What can you do?*

Read labels. Look, ask, enquire, find out about what you want to buy.

Don't buy so much! Ask yourself if you really need what you are buying.

Remember that boycotting a product doesn't necessarily mean going without. It can mean campaigning for something else.

Be positive – support small companies who produce environmentally sound goods.

Try using group consumer power. See the Introduction and the section on Groups at the end of the book.

Cotton

What's the point of wearing your Save the Planet T-shirts if the cotton is full of CHEMICALS and PESTICIDES? Cotton is commonly thought of as being a natural product, something that greens would wear. It is certainly more comfortable than some of the synthetic materials used for our clothes today. But there is increasing concern about the way cotton in the United States, China, Brazil and elsewhere is grown.

Most of that concern centres on the amounts of dangerous PESTICIDES and CHEMICALS that are sprayed on the cotton. In China and Brazil, 11 poisonous chemicals, all of which have been banned in most industrial countries and are on the United Nations Consolidation List of banned chemicals, have been found on cotton.

Cotton is a CASH CROP, and takes much-needed land away from local people in order to raise the money to pay off their country's debt. CHLORINE-based bleaches, chemicals and other substances used to treat cotton after it has been farmed also cause environmental problems.

■ *What can you do?*

Try to buy 'green cotton', which does not use any unnecessary chemicals. The chain store Next in the UK has just introduced a range.

Buy unbleached cotton whenever possible.

Avoid cotton and synthetic mixtures if you can, as it is more likely that bleaches and chemicals have been used to produce them.

Cycling

Save the world on two wheels! Cycling is a convenient, environmentally friendly way of getting around. For comparatively little effort and cost, you can get about without causing AIR POLLUTION or contributing to the GREENHOUSE EFFECT. It is the most energy-efficient form of transport in the world, giving about 360 km for the energy equivalent of one litre of petrol. The only energy it needs, of course, is your own, which comes from the food you eat. Cycling is a good way to stay fit and healthy.

There are many more good reasons for cycling, especially in cities. Because city traffic moves so slowly (sometimes less than 18 km per hour), bikes can actually get you to your destination faster. They are easy to park (12 bikes can be parked in the space that one car takes up), which helps ease parking congestion.

Bikes are cheaper to manufacture and buy than cars and more straightforward to maintain.

To be able to cycle safely requires care. CARS have always been the primary concern of transport planners. This means that cycle lanes, cycle paths off the main roads, signs for cyclists and bike-parking facilities in Britain are all rather few and far between. Cities are dangerous places for cyclists – 280 were killed on the roads in Britain in 1987. Countries like the Netherlands and Germany have done far more to enable their populations to cycle, and in Denmark 41 per cent of people travel to work by bike.

Many of today's cyclists have found that they want to campaign for better conditions for themselves and their bikes.

■ *What can you do?*

Can you ride a bike? Your school or youth centre may run the National Cycling Proficiency Test which is your first step to becoming a cyclist.

Buy a bike – a cycling shop or a cyclist friend should be able to advise you. *Richard's Bicycle Book* will help you choose. A bike soon pays for itself in the fares you save.

Buy a good cycling helmet and wear it. Until you are totally proficient it is better to get off the bike and walk it than to negotiate huge four-lane roundabouts. Remember that drivers might not control their vehicles as well as you do yours.

Contact the UK Cycle Campaign Network and the London Cycling Campaign.

If you are not satisfied with the provision for cyclists in your area, contact your local council (begin at the town hall). Find out whether they are taking account of cyclists in their traffic plans and schemes.

DDT

DDT (Dichloro-diphenyl-trichloroethane) is a powerful, artificially made CHEMICAL which kills insects. It was used all over the world from the 1930s onward as a PESTICIDE, until its use was banned, first in the USA in 1971 and thereafter in West Gemany, France and most industrial countries, after research showed that it was a powerful carcinogen (cancer-causing substance).

The banning of DDT in the '70s should have been the end of the story, but unfortunately it wasn't. DDT lasts for a long time in the environment. Birds were still found to have high levels of it in their bodies in the late 1980s.

The world as a whole is certainly not free of DDT. Some companies in the industrialised world are still manufacturing and exporting large quantities of DDT to the developing countries. The DDT is being used on CASH CROPS, which are then exported around the world. Pests seem to be developing a resistance to DDT, which means that more and more of it is needed to kill them. DDT is building up in humans, too: high levels of it have been found in the milk of many nursing mothers in the developing countries.

■ *What can you do?*

This is an issue where you can't act by yourself first.

Support the Pesticides Trust, which campaigns against British manufacturers of DDT who export it to the Third World.

You can write to these manufacturers yourself by finding out their names from the Pesticides Trust.

Don't buy other products made by these companies.

Deodorants

Have you got BO? We are paranoid about body odour: we buy millions of deodorants and antiperspirants every year to help mask the smell of our own bodies. They contain CHEMICALS that we probably don't need to be putting on ourselves, and their packaging, often in AEROSOLS, can be an environmental hazard, too.

Deodorants work by using an artificial fragrance to mask the smell of sweat. Antiperspirants work by blocking the pores in your armpits with the chemical aluminium chlorohydrate to stop you being able to perspire. Perspiring is an important body function which helps us to get rid of substances our bodies don't need. Many people are allergic to both deodorants and antiperspirants and they can generally irritate and harden the skin.

Many of the synthetic products used in deodorants and antiperspirants are also tested on animals (see ANIMAL TESTING).

▓ *What can you do?*

Some people perspire more than others. Wash daily if you can, and try going without deodorant or antiperspirant and see if it makes any difference at all!

Use cruelty-free products made from natural ingredients and not in aerosol packaging.

Try pure essential oils diluted in a scentless oil like almond or jojoba. Lavender, bergamot and grapefruit are all good, and cypress oil has a reputation for being excellent for sweaty feet. You can get essential oils from most health shops.

Try Karen Christensen's suggestion from *Home Ecology* – bicarbonate of soda patted on with cotton wool.

See also BEAUTY.

Deserts

Human intervention in the natural soil patterns of the world is making the deserts spread. All over the planet, land that was once fertile is being lost. Every year, an area of about 12 million hectares – larger than Britain – becomes arid and parched, with nothing to show that anything ever grew there.

'Desertification' is the technical term for the breakdown of fertile land into desert. There are four main reasons for desertification. The first is poor irrigation (artificial water supply), which makes the SOIL so salty it is difficult for crops to grow. The second is the land drying out after plants and trees have been slashed down, which also causes loss of HABITAT (see FORESTS, RAINFORESTS). When the trees are not there to hold water, rainfall patterns are affected where the forests once were and sometimes in other areas too. The third is overgrazing, where too many cattle flatten and destroy the vegetation (see MEAT). And the fourth is overcultivation, where land which would not naturally bear crops is cleared and ploughed in a desperate attempt to farm it (see AGRICULTURE). Any one of these four, when practised to excess, can turn previously productive land into desert.

The problem is made more acute by the fact that the lands that are affected by desertification are usually populated by poor people. Often, the governments of their countries will not or cannot step in to help them make the land produce again (rehabilitate the land), because this is not seen as being economic. Also, because of the world population rise, which is projected to increase, there are more people to feed and the land has to be worked harder, which just makes the problem worse.

■ *What can you do?*

You can't stop deserts spreading all on your own. Join a relief organisation like Green Deserts, who work in the northern Sudan, helping people to develop their own activities for keeping the desert back.

Or join Population Concern, who have health and family-planning education projects in deforested areas like Bangladesh.

Detergents

You probably hate doing the washing-up and you always need clothes hours before they go into the wash. Detergents are the sort of thing you never worry about, as long as they're in the cupboard. Detergents include washing powders, bath and kitchen cleaners and washing-up liquids. They contain CHEM- ICALS which may irritate our skins and which wash out into the water supply causing environmental damage and pollution.

Most detergents contain surfactants (surface active agents) and bleach. Surfactants separate fats and oils from the surfaces being cleaned. They can irritate skin and are even thought to contribute to cancer and birth defects. Bleach, once it washes into the water supply, can kill even the bacteria we need.

Washing powders can contain phosphates, optical bright- eners and enzymes. Phosphates, when they combine with the nitrates in our water supply from FERTILISERS, help algae, the tiny green plants in rivers and lakes, to grow. A rich green 'bloom' appears on the water and deprives fish of oxygen, so they die. The United States and Canada are so worried about this they have restricted phosphates in detergents.

Cleaning products sometimes contain a substance called NTA (nitro-tri-acetic acid), which combines with HEAVY METALS to form soluble compounds. This means that these metals, which would normally remain at the bottom of lakes and rivers, are reintroduced into the water supply. They can even end up in DRINKING WATER. Water companies in the Netherlands are showing great concern about the increased use of NTA.

Optical brighteners help products look white and enzymes break up protein stains like chocolate and egg, but both have been known to cause ALLERGIES.

In the late 1980s, detergent manufacturers became aware that their products could be dangerous. More and more 'environmentally friendly' cleaning products were made avail- able. Although some are more expensive than the usual cleaning products, they are far less damaging to the environment.

■ *What can you do?*

Encourage your parents to buy cleaning products such as those made by Ecover and Clearspring, who all have ranges of cleaners which damage the environment as little as possible.

Many supermarkets stock these, and you can buy them from health shops too.

Watch out for detergents in other products. Shampoo and bubble bath both contain detergents. Try to buy products like the Body Shop's shampoos, which contain sugar-based foaming agents.

Sometimes you can use your own alternatives to bottled cleaning products. Baking powder can clean kitchen surfaces, baths and sinks, and so can household soap – though you may have to scrub a bit harder. Ordinary table salt makes a good scouring powder and white distilled vinegar is good mixed half-and-half with water for cleaning glass, tiles and even toilets.

Dioxin

Dioxin is reputedly one of the most dangerous CHEMICALS known. It is thought to be 50,000 times more poisonous than cyanide. Although dioxin is known to be very dangerous to animals, scientists do not agree about its effect on human beings.

Dioxin is the artificial product of a chemical reaction. It is usually found when chemicals like CHLORINE are used in industrial processes. Tiny quantities of dioxin are formed as a by-product of these processes, completely by accident. Dioxins have caused cancers and birth defects in many animals and birds. They are not BIODEGRADABLE, which means they can last for a very long time in the environment.

Dioxins are produced when PLASTIC is burned and in chemical combustion processes, such as when iron or steel are made. Dioxins can also be found in leaded petrol; in bleached white PAPER products, including food wrappings; SANITARY PRODUCTS and writing paper; and in weedkillers (herbicides) like Agent Orange (2–4T), which were used in Vietnam and more recently in South Africa.

The name 'dioxin' usually refers to one particular form of this chemical – 2, 3, 7, 8 TCDD, which is the most dangerous. In quantities smaller than a millionth of a millionth of a gramme, TCDD can harm wildlife. It accumulates in the body fat of animals and humans, and it is generally thought wise to avoid any possible contamination from dioxin.

■ *What can you do?*

Avoid whiter-than-white paper products. Buy the ones marked 'unbleached' or 'non-chlorine bleached' instead.

Avoid smoking CIGARETTES, which contain dioxins in the tobacco and in the bleached white paper.

Use unleaded petrol in your family's car and encourage your friends to go unleaded (see LEAD).

Try to avoid products which have had chemicals used on them. See if you can buy ORGANIC instead.

By finding other uses for PLASTICS you buy instead of just throwing them away, you can indirectly cut down on the amount of dioxins being produced by incineration of WASTE.

Write to the manufacturers of the white paper products you buy and ask them to provide all their paper goods chlorine-free.

Direct Action

Direct action is anything done by environmentalists or other pressure groups (see GREEN PEOPLE) that directly affects, stops or interferes with the activity the action is protesting against. For example, a group might take direct action to stop trees being cut down by climbing up them and staying there, or an individual might take direct action by refusing to pay a bill from a polluting or environmentally bad company.

Greenpeace have become world-famous for their direct actions. They stop whalers killing whales by putting their small boats between the whales and their hunters. They publicise nuclear-waste dumping by blocking the waste pipe. But direct action is not only effective when organised by very large groups. In Humberside and Lincolnshire groups of young people blocked the road to a potential nuclear-waste site by just refusing to move. Women at Greenham Common used direct action to protest against nuclear missiles. They tried to stop convoys leaving the American base there on practice manoeuvres and gained massive publicity.

In many parts of Britain young people have used direct action to stop fox hunts by blocking the hunters' routes.

■ *What can you do?*

If you decide that direct action is a good way for your campaign to get the message across, do remember these simple rules:

> always be non-violent
> try to win the sympathy of local people and the person or company you oppose
> plan well in advance
> get legal advice if possible
> make sure that the action is taken with care and good humour
> only do it if it is actually relevant to the cause

Support organisations like Greenpeace and the League Against Cruel Sports.

'Disposable'

Today you can buy 'disposable' knickers, cameras, plates and even a wedding dress. Around the mid-1950s, factories became much more mechanised and 'efficient'. Industrialists came up with the idea of making products people could throw away, and the 'throw-away' mentality, which has since spread worldwide, was created. Everything became 'flushable' or 'disposable'. Cars were designed with 'built-in obsolescence', meaning they would need replacing after a set period of time. Suddenly, nothing seemed built to last.

It is only now, in the nineties, that we are reaping the dire consequences of that mentality. The things we dispose of do not actually disappear – they simply go somewhere else. Our SEAS and rivers are becoming polluted and filthy with the WASTE we throw away every day. Birds and fish are dying, caught up in litter. Our town streets are waste dumps and our LANDFILL SITES are leaking.

We buy 340 million boxes of paper tissues a year in Britain. If we were to use cotton handkerchiefs instead, it would reduce the number of trees cut down and the pollution caused by the poisonous process involved in the manufacture of tissues, and there would be less waste to dispose of.

Every year over 25 million cars are discarded as junk. If they lasted twice as long, that huge pile of scrap would be halved.

We are simply throwing away goods that cost dearly, both in terms of the processes needed to make them and the waste they create. We need to think of goods in terms of their environmental as well as their monetary cost. RECYCLING is better than throwing away.

■ *What can you do?*

Try not to buy 'disposable' things. See if you can find substitutes, like cloth towels for paper kitchen towels, or plastic containers instead of clingfilm.

Think seriously about buying second-hand instead of new. This is perhaps the most direct way of making sure that products are used for all the time they will last. It's cheaper, too!

If you buy new, try if you can to get a product which will last as long as possible, even if it is a bit more expensive.

Try not to throw out things you don't need any more. Give them to friends or charities instead. Some countries even have a 'street sale' where, about once every two months, everyone puts the things they don't need outside their doors and people stroll around 'shopping' from the doorsteps.

Buy rechargeable BATTERIES, or avoid batteries whenever you can.

Dolphins

Dolphins are a species loved by human beings. Friendly and intelligent, they have been known to help drowning sailors. Despite this, over 400,000 dolphins are killed worldwide each year.

Dolphins die as a result of conflict with the world fishing industry. Schools of tuna swim underneath dolphins, and when fishermen drop their nets to catch the tuna, the dolphins become entangled in the nets and are dragged under water and drowned. The situation is particularly bad in the eastern tropical Pacific, where as many as 250,000 dolphins may be killed each year. Different types of nets, with sonic devices to warn the dolphins, could do a lot to lower these figures, but so far no real steps have been taken.

In Japan and Peru, and on a smaller scale in areas like Greenland and the Danish Faroe Islands, dolphins are hunted and killed for meat at the rate of about 230,000 per year.

Dolphins are hunted by fishermen who believe they eat too many fish. As our SEAS become more filthy, they are also being poisoned. At least 50 per cent of the population of bottle-nosed dolphins along the east coast of the USA has died off, with pollution the major cause.

Dolphins are also hunted for zoos and for research. They are even used by the US navy to plant underwater mines, for example. It is thought that the Soviet Union also has a military dolphin programme.

■ *What can you do?*

Try to find out where your tuna comes from. The Whale and Dolphin Conservation Society, or organisations like Greenpeace or the World Wide Fund for Nature will be able to tell you. You may wish to boycott the product and tell the manufacturers why.

Join one of these organisations and support their work for dolphin protection.

Drinking Water

We may think that the water coming out of our taps is safe to drink, but environmental groups have shown that it is, instead, a cocktail of chemicals. Tap water in Britain has been found to contain nitrates from FERTILISERS, aluminium, PESTICIDES, and LEAD from old water pipes.

Nitrates come from the various fertilisers used on the land and from grasslands being ploughed up. They have been connected with the 'blue baby syndrome' (see FERTILISERS) and with stomach cancer. In 1989 at least 1.7 million people in Britain consumed water that broke European limits for nitrates.

Aluminium is thought to cause Alzheimer's disease, a

degenerative disease of the brain. It is added to water at treatment works in the form of aluminium sulphate, which stops the water looking brown. Two million people in Britain had drinking water which exceeded the aluminium level permitted by the European Community according to a study in 1989.

The two pesticides most commonly found in tap water are Atrazine and Simazine, which have caused tumours in rats. Atrazine is forbidden in West Germany, and Simazine is currently under review by the World Health Organisation. Nearly 300 water sources in Britain contained pesticides above the level set by the European Community in 1989.

Well over 2 million people in the UK are drinking water contaminated with lead from household pipes more than 15 years old. Lead damages children's brains and can even poison babies before they are born. A proposal in 1980 to get rid of all lead plumbing in British homes was not passed by the government, who instead began adding chemcals to water to stop it absorbing so much lead.

Other CHEMICALS are also polluting the water supply. Trihalomethanes, a form of chloroform, are created when CHLORINE used to kill bacteria in water at treatment works reacts with organic material such as peat in water from moorland reservoirs and lowland rivers. They are thought to cause cancer, particularly of the bladder and bowel, and they have been turning up in water all over the south of England.

■ What can you do?

Filter your drinking water. You can use either a jug with a filter or an attachment for your taps. But this should only be a short-term measure – we should be demanding clean water to drink!

Write to the Department of the Environment asking what they plan to do to cut down contamination of drinking water.

Join an environmental organisation to campaign for cleaner water.

Dry-Cleaning

After you've spent all day Saturday looking for that perfect outfit, suddenly someone spills a drink over you. Only then do you read the label – dry-clean only.

Dry-cleaning uses chemical solvents instead of water to clean the clothes. The two most common CHEMICALS used are trichlorofluoroethylene and perchloroethylene. Not only are they both poisonous, but one is a chlorofluorocarbon (see CFCS). Effects from short-term exposure to them include nausea, giddiness and even unconsciousness. Some customers have passed out after driving away with still-damp dry-cleaned clothes in their cars. Long-term exposure leads to the accumulation of the compounds in the body, causing organ damage and an increased risk of cancer.

The chemicals affect other people too. A government report shows that the drinking water of up to 1.5 million British people could be contaminated with them.

■ *What can you do?*

If you have clothes which need dry-cleaning, hang them outdoors or in an unoccupied room when you get them home from the cleaners so the chemicals can disperse.

If you are using a self-service machine, make sure the clothes are totally dry when the cycle is finished, and if they are not, close the machine and call the manager. Don't overload the machine.

You can try handwashing 'dry-clean only' clothes made with natural fabrics like silk and cotton. They are likely to be all right if you wash them very gently and use pure soap rather than a biological cleaner.

Try not to buy clothes with 'dry-clean only' labels.

Ecology

The word 'ecology' comes from the Greek *oikos*, 'home' or 'habitat', and *logos*, 'study'. It means looking at and studying all the relationships and interactions between a living thing and its environment. In this sense, ecology is different from study of the environment, which is more related to the state of the planet and the disasters it is facing.

Ecology and ecological subjects are included on many school courses: geography, science and social-studies courses cover various aspects of ecology. To read further about the subject, see the book list in the back of this book.

■ *What can you do?*

If you are interested in the subject, see if one of your school courses has an ecology-related option you can take.

In 1989, the London Ecology Centre was planning a secondary-schools membership scheme, which you could join with a group from your school. They also have information about ecology in general.

Elephants

Did you know that some religions still worship elephants? Elephants live in India and in Africa. They are social animals, who live in large herds led by an older female. Elephants appear to have a close and loving family life, with baby elephants being cared for by the whole herd until they are old enough to break away and form herds of their own.

Between 1985 and 1989, 89,000 elephants were killed for their tusks by poachers who supply international dealers with ivory (see JEWELLERY). Elephant hunters use automatic rifles and whole families are wiped out at a time. The male (or 'bull') elephants' tusks are hacked off for the ivory and the baby elephants are left to starve or be eaten by lions.

Elephants are becoming an ENDANGERED SPECIES. If we do not act now, there is a very strong possibility that they will be extinct by the mid-1990s.

Elephants are one of the world's most majestic animals. We must not let them die.

■ *What can you do?*

Refuse to buy ivory in any of its forms.

Write to Zoo Check for details of their Ivory Out campaign.

Join the Environmental Investigation Agency, who have exposed the recent elephant scandals, or the World Wide Fund for Nature. Animal Aid and Elefriends also have information on the subject.

Endangered Species

About 1,000 species of animals (and 25,000 species of plants) are facing extinction. Only a very small proportion of these are becoming naturally extinct – that is, dying out slowly over a period of time because they cannot adapt themselves to changes in the environment. The majority are becoming extinct because of human intervention: people wanting to profit from animals in some way, usually by selling their skin, oil, meat, hides, shells and so on. Extinction occurs when beings are competing with wild animals for living space and when animals are killed for enjoyment.

People also trade in living wild animals, for instance exotic birds like parrots, macaws and lovebirds. It is estimated that 10 million birds each year are caught and exported. The birds are netted and stuffed in tubes, and half of them die of fright, exhaustion and lack of air before they even leave the country. Four out of five die before they reach their destination, and most of the survivors die within one year.

Humans are also responsible for 'indirect extinction' – that is, destroying a plant's or an animal's HABITAT. An example of this is in Indonesia, where the cultivation of durian fruit has given way to the cultivation of rice to feed the growing population. A species of bat used to feed on the durian, and now that species is dying. Thousands of species of plant also become extinct when land is turned over to AGRICULTURE, including plants that could have real importance as cures for many of our illnesses (see RAINFORESTS).

The prospects for species that are endangered today – this includes ELEPHANTS, rhinos, cheetahs and snow leopards – are not good. The human population is increasing by one million people every six days. Habitat like the rainforests is being cut down to grow food for humans: over 2,000 sq km per day worldwide are lost. Trade in furs, skins, hides, horn and ivory continues, and the animals are simply being killed off.

■ *What can you do?*

Avoid buying animal souvenirs – turtle shells, skins, ivory – and try to convince other people not to buy them either (see also JEWELLERY).

Make sure you know which products come from animals, particularly endangered species, and try to avoid buying them.

Debate the moral difficulties surrounding endangered-species protection versus human needs.

Join an organisation concerned with endangered species and wildlife. Greenpeace, the Royal Society for the Protection of Birds, the World Wide Fund for Nature and the Young People's Trust for Endangered Species are good bets (the last has a Young Environmentalist of the Year award, too). This will make you more aware of which of the products we buy come from endangered species.

Consider campaigning outside shops selling furs or animal souvenirs.

See also WHALES, DOLPHINS, ZOOS.

Energy Conservation

Readily available energy in the form of coal, oil and gas is so much a part of our lives that we hardly think about it any more. In affluent consumer societies like the UK, we use up to 50 times as much energy as someone living in a developing country.

But it doesn't come free. Our lifestyle is powered mostly by FOSSIL FUELS (coal, oil and gas) and smaller amounts of NUCLEAR POWER. The burning of fossil fuels is causing AIR POLLUTION and ACID RAIN and adds to the GREENHOUSE EFFECT. Nuclear power produces other hazards such as RADIATION leaks and nuclear waste.

Finding other sources of energy (see RENEWABLE ENERGY) is one solution, but we can help even more by cutting down the excessive amount we use in the first place. Energy conservation is really about doing more with less. For example, if every household in the UK were to fit energy-efficient lightbulbs, we wouldn't have to build any more nuclear power stations. If we insulated our homes better and fitted draught excluders, we could cut down the amount of pollution produced from heating our homes by more than 30 per cent. Some houses are so badly insulated that they might as well have a six-inch hole through the wall!

Everyone should be able to save energy in some way, and it is one of the most direct and positive ways to save the planet.

■ *What can you do?*

You can start at home by turning off unnecessary lights and heating. Close doors and windows to help keep the heat in. Get your parents to fit draught excluders around doors and letter boxes, or fit them yourself.

Ask your family if the water heater needs to be on all the time. Does it have a thermostat? Can you turn the temperature down?

Can you share a source of energy? If a group of friends wants to watch the same TV programme, why not all watch the same television set?

Is your house properly insulated? You may be able to help your family save lots of money if it isn't. Local libraries and council offices usually have information with ideas for draught-proofing doors and windows, fitting thermostats to radiators and insulating lofts. You can even fit solar panels to your house. Neighbourhood Energy Action run several hundred practical schemes where you can learn and see a house being insulated for yourself.

If your family are buying new appliances like washing machines, TV sets or fridges, try to encourage them to ask for the energy-efficient models now on the market.

Write to the Centre for Alternative Technology for information on energy conservation. You can visit them if you are near Wales. They have a house which runs on solar power and windmills. Even a bionic loo.

E Numbers

E numbers are an official form of labelling for food ADDITIVES. The E prefix before the number shows that the additive has been passed for use by the European Economic Community.

E numbers fall into seven basic groups. A prefix E1 followed by two numbers means the additive is a colour. E2 stands for PRESERVATIVES. E3 additives are mostly antioxidants, used to make sure that fat in foods does not go off and taste rancid; synergists, which accentuate the antioxidising capability of other substances in the foods; and colour preservatives, which make sure food colour does not fade. E4 are stabilisers which help things to set and become thick; the E4 list also includes some sweetening agents. E5 are acids and alkalis, used to affect flavours and to prevent substances from caking – going into lumps.

Some additives on the market have numbers without the E prefix, which means that the European Economic Community has not passed them for safety. A number beginning with 6 means the additive is a flavour enhancer, used to heighten the flavour of foods. There are no numbers beginning with 7 and 8, but numbers beginning with 9 are glazes and polishes, and from 920 up are 'improving' agents. Additive 925 is CHLORINE, used in small quantities for bleaching flour.

Not all additives are dangerous. E300 is vitamin C, and E322 is lecithin, which works to prevent fat from separating and is actually nutritious. But some additives do appear to be dangerous. E102 (tartrazine), an orange-yellow colour, is one of several additives that have been connected to hyperactivity in children. E123 (amaranth) has been shown to cause cancerous tumours in rats. Additive 621 is monosodium glutamate, a flavour enhancer and meat tenderiser which in some people has caused hot flushes, dizziness and headache.

The difficulty, of course, is knowing which additives to avoid. Maurice Hanssen, the author of *E for Additives*, gives a list of 57 which he suggests should not be eaten.

We can cut down on the quantity of additive-containing foods we eat. That basically means steering clear of packets and tins and instead buying fresh (though fresh food, too, may have been interfered with – see PESTICIDES, IRRADIATION). ORGANIC food is a good option, but it is expensive.

■ *What can you do?*

See our suggestions under ADDITIVES.

Buy a food directory like *E for Additives* and play detective. You might want to do a project on food additives, investigating which ones are known to have had bad effects on people and animals, and which foods they tend to turn up in.

Factory Farming

Factory farming is the raising of animals specifically for food. Chickens, pigs and cattle are three of the main species factory farmed in Britain. For many years now animal rights campaigners have been protesting against the cruelty of the methods which are used.

Chickens are farmed both for their eggs and their meat. Eight out of ten eggs eaten in Britain come from battery hens – birds kept in cages where they cannot spread their wings or turn around. Often their beaks are amputated, and the lights burn for seventeen hours a day to keep them laying. They are prone to diseases like salmonella, and many hens die. Eggs can be laid against the bodies of dead or dying birds.

Broiler chickens – the ones we eat – are raised in huge sheds. Up to 100,000 birds may be huddled together in one building. Broiler chickens are slaughtered at seven weeks old, and we eat 500 million of them in Britain every year.

Pigs, too, are factory farmed. They lie on concrete or on slatted floors, and 60% of the breeding sows in the UK are kept in metal-barred tiestalls, where they are forced to lie in their own excrement. The sows give birth in narrow 'farrowing crates' with no bedding instead of the nests of leaves they would naturally build for their young. Sows are required to have five litters every two years and after giving birth they are often mated again before their milk has dried up.

Piglets are kept in piglet battery cages similar to those used for hens. They are often reared in darkness or semi-darkness until they are moved to special 'fattening pens'. Many of these are so automated that the pigs are fed by a machine which scatters food over them, although others do have space for the pigs to exercise outside. They are slaughtered at seven months old, and in Britain we consume more than 15.5 million pigs a year.

Cattle are reared both for meat and milk. Dairy cows are milked by machine twice a day and are kept regularly pregnant to ensure their milk supply will not dry up. Often they are fed protein concentrates made from animal products and because cows would not normally eat meat, the protein can make them lame or even give them brain diseases. Cows can also be injected with HORMONES to increase their milk yield.

Beef cattle, although they are kept in fields, have their diets altered. They are fattened quickly on barley so they can be killed at eleven months old. Calves are kept in small wooden crates and fed a special liquid diet to keep their meat, called veal, white. By the time they are slaughtered they can hardly move in their crates.

■ *What can you do?*

Try to cut down on the meat you are eating. See VEGETARIAN and vegan for some ideas, or write to the Vegetarian Society.

Try to buy animal products that are humanely farmed. Many supermarkets now stock free-range eggs or chicken. These come from birds who have been allowed access to space in which they can run around. The Real Meat Company and the Pure Meat Company supply meat from animals raised humanely. While these products are more expensive than the factory farmed ones, you could try cooking a cheap vegetarian meal once a week to make up the difference in price.

Join any of the animal welfare organisations at the back of the book. Compassion in World Farming and Animal Aid are two, but there are many others.

See also MEAT.

Fast Food

'Fast food' is cooked food we buy ready to eat. It includes hamburgers, fish and chips, hot dogs, and pizzas. The UK fast-food market alone is worth £1.5 billion – that is hundreds of millions of take-away meals.

Because fast food is so convenient – you can buy a relatively cheap meal in two minutes – huge numbers of people eat it regularly. Of those, many people, particularly those who are short of money, have found that they can base their whole diet around the afternoon hamburger or the evening pizza. But eating like this could be damaging their health and the health of the planet.

Fast food is not well balanced nutritionally. It is low in protein and essential vitamins, but high in fat, sugar and salt. Basing a diet around fast foods is very likely to make us malnourished, even though we may gain weight because of all the extra calories. Fast food also contains many ADDITIVES.

A '100 per cent beefburger' can legally be 30 per cent fat – an 'economy' beefburger can be over 40 per cent fat. Fat is added to sausages, pies and pasties, too – and that's before any cooking in fat.

Sugar is in pizzas, spare ribs, sausage rolls and sweet and sour sauce, as well as in milkshakes and soft drinks (about seven teaspoons in a small cola).

Salt is added to raw MEAT mixtures in large quantities.

The chemical additives are colourings (for example, in fish batter), artificial sweeteners (in pickles), emulsifiers, antioxidants, flour improvers and thickening agents (see E NUMBERS).

Even the meat used can be dubious. The law permits using all sorts of offal (internal organs and intestines) and meat that has been mechanically recovered (see HAMBURGERS), which comes from all over the animal.

If fast food were labelled with what it contains, we could make an informed choice about what we are eating. But fast-food manufacturers do not legally have to label their products.

Fast food is a global concern. The fast-food industry uses large amounts of meat. Beef production requires extensive land, and much of this land is in areas where RAINFORESTS are being burned down so more cattle can be farmed.

As fast food spreads around the world, it affects the diets of the people who buy it. In Japan, where fast food has become a fad, studies show that the previously healthy population are showing signs of fat-related heart complaints.

Fast-food containers create a huge amount of WASTE and are really only used for a few seconds. The average meal from a hamburger chain will have a PAPER wrapper and a box for the burger, a container for the fries, a paper cup for the milkshake and a paper napkin, all wrapped up in a paper bag. None of the paper is recycled. Some hamburger boxes – those rigid polystyrene containers – are made with CFCs, which destroy the OZONE LAYER.

Fast food may be fun, tasty and convenient, but it certainly has a high cost both to our health and to the planet.

■ What can you do?

Try cutting down on the amount of fast food you are eating.

See if you can think up a quick meal that could replace a fast-food meal. It might not be quite as convenient – but scrambled eggs or baked beans and toast cooked at home give you more nutrition and cost the planet far less.

See if you can stop eating fast food altogether after a while. If you can, write to the manager of your local fast-food outlet and say why you aren't buying it any more.

Write to the major chains and complain about their over-packaging. Ask them what their food contains, too.

Fertilisers

Fertilisers are used all over the world to ensure that crops are produced in as large quantities as possible. Natural fertilisers like manure and guano (bird dung) were in the past used to help crops grow, but the crops of today rely on artificial fertilisers.

Artificial fertilisers contain nitrates. These are nitrogen compounds. They can dramatically increase crop yield. Fig-ures suggest that more than twice as many crops can be produced from artificially fertilised land. Because of a growing world population and the spread of modern farming methods, many farmers are now becoming dependent on artificial fertilisers to meet crop demands.

The nitrogen that is not absorbed by crops is washed out of the SOIL and into rivers and lakes by the rain. It then fertilises the algae and weeds which grow there. These small plants begin to grow excessively, darkening the water and destroying the natural balance of rivers and lakes so that plants and fish die.

Nitrates are taken in by the human body through water and food and changed into substances called nitrosamines, which are thought to be carcinogenic (cancer-causing). Some of the DRINKING WATER in Great Britain has been found to contain high levels of nitrates, which is particularly risky for babies. The 'blue baby syndrome', when babies suddenly stop breathing, turn blue and can die, is thought to be linked to high levels of nitrate in drinking water.

Some of the nitrogen in fertilisers contributes to the GREEN-HOUSE EFFECT. In the atmosphere, the nitrogen becomes nitrous oxide, one of the greenhouse gases.

At the moment, farming is difficult without fertilisers. Finding alternatives will not happen overnight, but in the meantime, we can try to avoid nitrates and support companies that produce their food without the use of fertilisers which contain them.

■ *What can you do?*

Try growing your own vegetables. You can use natural fertilisers such as compost (see GARDENING) – you can make this yourself. Compost slowly releases nutrients into the soil.

If your pocket will permit it buy ORGANIC vegetables and fruit. They are grown without artificial fertilisers and taste good too.

Forests

Forests are essential to life on the planet. They keep the earth's water balance stable by holding water in their roots. This helps SOIL to stay in position, preventing it from becoming dry and washing or blowing away, preventing flooding, such as has recently occurred in Bangladesh, where no trees are left to stop the rain washing away crops. Forests also help prevent the spread of DESERTS.

Forests provide homes for thousands of animals, plants, birds and insects. A natural forest houses a complex ecosystem

– a mini-society of various creatures and plants all interacting together in the same HABITAT.

We are destroying our forest at a rate more than seven times greater than we are replanting them. We are chopping down trees to meet our demand for land for farming and raising cattle for MEAT. We are using huge quantities of wood for PAPER. In this way, we are affecting the climate balance on the planet. We are helping to cause floods and destruction. We are depriving rare species of their homes and even sometimes making them extinct (see ENDANGERED SPECIES).

As well as destroying forests, we are also making it more difficult for the ones that are left to survive. Many European and North American forests have already been weakened by ACID RAIN. Forests are struggling to cope with the climate changes on their way as a result of the GREENHOUSE EFFECT. Tree diseases are becoming widespread.

We need to stop putting pressure on our forests. One of the answers that has been suggested is to plant sustainable forests – planned forests, in which more trees are planted for every tree cut down. This will, at least, help meet our demand for wood products and PAPER. But a planted forest won't hold the complicated ecosystems of a natural forest.

■ *What can you do?*

Try to reduce your use of paper products. Read the section on PAPER for ideas.

Plant trees yourself. You can join and support organisations that plant trees around the world, like the Men of the Trees, or locally, like the Woodland Trust. Or you can work with schemes like those run by the British Trust for Conservation Volunteers.

Find out about the trees in your area. Is there an area of trees which developers want to cut down? Can you help to prevent this by joining up with other people in your area? Read your local paper and see what is happening.

Read the section on RAINFORESTS to find out how you can act to help save tropical forests being destroyed.

Fossil Fuels

Fossil fuels are the fossilised remains of plants and animals, laid down in the earth over millions of years. They form rocks and gases which we can use to produce fuel like oil to generate electricity and power our machines.

Oil and gas are often found in rocks that contain arched shapes, where pockets of gases rise to the top of the rock formation. Oil and gas are found mostly in Canada, the Middle East, Nigeria, the Soviet Union, Venezuela and the USA. The production of oil and gas is already thought to have peaked in the UK and is slowing down.

Coal is found mainly in China, the Soviet Union and western Europe.

Approximately 30 per cent of the energy we get from fossil fuels is wasted even before we use it in its conversion to useful energy and it causes environmental problems in the process. ACID RAIN and the GREENHOUSE EFFECT are problems directly caused by our burning and using fossil fuels. This releases carbon dioxide into the environment along with a cocktail of other chemicals, including nitrous oxides and hydrocarbons.

Worldwide, we are using fossil fuels at an alarming rate. This source of energy took millions of years to create – we will have used it up in just a few decades. At the present rate of consumption we have enough oil for the next 60–80 years, enough coal for the next 150 years and enough natural gas for the next 50 years. In the history of the planet this is not a long time and with all our advances in technology we should be exploring RENEWABLE ENERGY and using energy more efficiently (see ENERGY CONSERVATION).

Indirect problems caused by fossil fuels include mining accidents, oil spills and gas explosions. The Alaskan oil spill from the Exxon Valdez caused the deaths of thousands of birds, fish, and mammals in 1989 and will affect wildlife in the area for decades. When an oil rig in the North Sea (Piper Alpha) blew up in 1988, many people were killed or wounded.

■ *What can you do?*

See under ENERGY CONSERVATION and RENEWABLE ENERGY.

Do a project or questionnaire for your friends to find out how much you know about fossil fuels and the energy that we use.

Gaia

The earth hangs in space, surrounded by a thin layer of atmosphere. From a distance, it looks like a blue, misty pearl. It is unique. No other planet in the solar system possesses exactly the same blend of gases to create life as we know it.

The biosphere – it means 'the sphere where life exists' – is the thin layer that includes the lower atmosphere, the oceans and the soil which supports all life. It seems to sustain itself by a complex combination of different systems and cycles. Climate patterns, the cycles of energy, ocean currents, winds and hundreds of other systems all work together, making life possible.

The idea that everything that lives on the planet is linked together is called the Gaia hypothesis (theory). This hypothesis has been developed by Dr James Lovelock, a British scientist, though it has been part of religious stories and myths for thousands of years. We know now that this planet and all that happens on it are interconnected.

One way to think of the planet is as a human body – made up mostly of water, with differing functions for different parts of the body. A Scottish scientist in the eighteenth-century, James Hutton, described the planet as a 'superorganism' when he compared the movements of the soil through plants and animals in the carbon cycle to the movements of blood flowing and circulating around the human body.

If the planet is like a human body, she can also be sick, and the pollution, waste, radioactivity, chemicals and dangerous gases emitted from industrial proceses all contribute to the sickness. Understanding Gaia means understanding that the survival of the plants, trees and wildlife which live on this planet with us is crucial to our own survival. The planet would not have created the substances that now threaten her survival. People have caused the problems facing us, so people must help to heal the planet for the future.

We've used 'she' to refer to the planet and Gaia because early stories about the beginning of the earth use the term 'Mother' for the planet, which is seen as a place where things are born, brought forth and grow, rather like a baby in a mother's womb. The first images in religion and art devoted to the Earth Mother appeared some 30,000 years ago, and relics and statues can be found all over the world.

■ *What can you do?*

Almost every section in this book will help you live in greater harmony with the planet. You can also read more about Gaia in the books on the reading list.

Gardening

One great way to go green is to start with your garden – or, if you don't have one, a box on your windowsill or even some houseplants. You will have the knowledge that a section of your own environment is totally 'green'. As a bonus, it will be a pleasure to look at and may even provide some good ORGANIC things to eat.

■ *What can you do?*

You can start on your windowsill. Fill yoghurt or cottage-cheese tubs with garden soil and drop seeds into them. Orange, apple and lemon pips grow well and make pretty trees, although you won't get fruit. Grape seeds grow into little vines. Avocado and mango stones will sprout, and you can even try planting conkers or acorns.

You can plant bulbs from gardening shops in bowls. If you plant them in potting compost in September, you will have flowers by Christmas.

If you have a garden, then the sky's the limit! Ask your parents for a plot of your own to grow things in. You could plant all kinds of vegetables and flowers. Try your local library for books on how to plan your garden.

Gardening green means using natural products to help you make your plants grow. That means no CHEMICAL plant foods or FERTILISERS. You can make your own fertiliser by picking nettles (use gloves) and packing them into a bucket or tub. Fill it with water and cover it, and in two weeks you will have a great (although a bit smelly) liquid food for all your plants.

Don't buy PESTICIDES. Bicarbonate of soda can get rid of mildew if you mix it up two grammes to a litre of water, and soapy water will kill greenfly.

Make your own gardening compost. This has the advantage of using up some of your kitchen WASTE, and saves buying peat from shops which is damaging the local ecosystem.

Contact the Soil Association or the Henry Doubleday Research Institute to find out more about organic gardening.

Greenhouse Effect

One of the most terrifying new problems to confront the planet is the greenhouse effect, or global warming.

The heat of the planet is trapped by the atmosphere in the same way a greenhouse traps heat in its glass walls and stops it escaping. But we are upsetting the natural process that has been going on for millions of years, by the way we live, with the result that the planet is now getting hotter. This won't just lead to a warmer climate. It will raise sea levels by expanding the oceans and melting the polar icecaps, lead to more extreme weather conditions like storms and droughts, and cause infestations of pests and insects.

We boost the greenhouse effect by the gases we produce. The main 'greenhouse gases' are:

carbon dioxide (50 per cent) which comes from FOSSIL FUELS such as coal and oil; CARS' exhausts; cutting down tropical RAINFORESTS and other FORESTS; and burning wood

methane (18 per cent) which is produced by cattle, who emit it from both ends; rice paddies; rotting organic matter in refuse tips; and the burning of wood, other vegetation and fossil fuels

nitrous oxide (6 per cent) from fossil-fuel combustion (burning); FERTILISERS, used for growing food; wood burning; and animal and human excreta

CFCs (14 per cent) which is a human invention, mostly found in propellants for aerosols; foam blowers; foam trays and boxes; foam mattresses and refrigerators

surface ozone (12 per cent) which is not the ozone layer but the ozone molecules that drop from the upper atmosphere in reaction to pollutants such as methane, carbon monoxide and nitrogen oxides, which mainly come from car-exhaust pollution

Some of these are naturally occurring gases, but the sophisticated technology used by humans is increasing the amounts of these gases in the atmosphere. The natural balance of the planet is being affected and the earth is beginning to heat up.

This 'overheating' could have disastrous effects. These include:

The melting of the polar icecaps. An increase of 5 per cent in the earth's overall heat could melt the Arctic icecap completely, raising the level of the world's seas.

Coastal flooding. As the world's seas rise, low-lying countries will be very badly affected. Countries like the Netherlands, the Maldives and Bangladesh could largely disappear.

The world's climate will change as the heat affects the natural climate patterns. We can expect more and more freak weather like tornados, floods, droughts and hurricanes.

Warmer weather in normally cool or temperate areas could lead to infestations of insects and droughts.

The world food-growing pattern will change. Disrupted climate means that crops might not grow when we expect or need them and rainfall will not be soaked up. Food supplies will become unpredictable and there may well be shortages.

Plants and animals will have trouble adapting to the new conditions as their HABITATS change. Some species will have to move to survive and others may even become extinct.

The greenhouse effect is recognised as a serious crisis and much research is devoted to it. It will take world action to deal with the greenhouse effect, but there are many basic things every single person can do to help reduce it.

■ *What can you do?*

Avoid CFCs in aerosols, packaging and refrigerators. Encourage your family to use fewer paint sprays, de-icers, hairsprays and air fresheners.

Buy and use a bike if you can (see CYCLING).

Use PUBLIC TRANSPORT if you can. It is far less polluting than private cars.

Save PAPER, which also helps to save the FORESTS, and use recycled paper as often as possible.

Eat less MEAT, particularly red meat from methane-producing cattle.

Save energy – make sure that the heat we create in our power stations doesn't just get lost. Even switching off lights helps. See ENERGY CONSERVATION for more ideas.

Help save the forests. Trees soak up some of the carbon dioxide we are producing. Don't buy tropical hardwoods (see RAINFORESTS). Support or join campaigns to save the forests, even plant trees yourself. Often your local council will provide trees if you provide the workforce. Contact the Woodland Trust, too – they plant trees for £1 each.

Contact the World Wide Fund for Nature, Greenpeace and Friends of the Earth for more information on the greenhouse effect.

Green People

Green people are everywhere – you meet them on the streets all the time: 'Oh, I never use aerosols any more' or 'We've changed to lead-free petrol so we're green now!' You can also meet people who have dedicated their lives to environmental action, like the women in the CHIPKO movement in India.

Most people agree that green people are those who care about the environment, they are more aware of environmental problems and they actually try to change things. Green people include political parties, pressure groups, consumers and worried parents. Here is a quick guide to green people to help you understand who they are:

Political parties

The Green Party is the real green political party. It has about 20,000 members in Britain but in the 1989 European Elections a lot more people – about 15 per cent of the British population – voted Green Party. The Green Party's manifesto encourages a reverence for the earth; protection of the environment; a healthy society; rights for future generations; RENEWABLE ENERGY and open democracy. You can get their full manifesto from their Party headquarters.

The main political parties, the Conservatives, Labour and Liberal Democrats, all have environment policies as they relate to pollution, energy and food. Some are better than others, but the 'greening' of the political parties has meant that they will be taking environmental issues far more seriously in the 1990s. Write to them all and ask for their environment policies and decide for yourself.

Environment groups

Pressure groups like **Greenpeace** and **Friends of the Earth** are what most people know as environmentalists. They try and effect change by encouraging political groups to change policies; by consumer action so that people buy non-damaging products; and by exposing industry and companies that have bad practices. Lists of some environmental pressure groups can be found at the back of the book. There are about 1,400 groups – so they are not all listed!

Eco-feminists

Eco-feminists believe that the world needs to be rebalanced and that a male-dominated society has encouraged the overuse and exploitation of the earth's resources. Women in the **Chipko** movement in India are considered eco-feminists, as are the members of the **Women's Environmental Network**.

Specialist groups

The **National Trust**, the **RSPB** (Royal Society for the Protection of Birds) and many other groups specialise in one particular campaign, like the protection of birds or nature reserves. Several million people in Britain are members of at least one such organisation.

Animal activists

Groups like **Animal Aid** and **BUAV** (the British Union for the Abolition of Vivisection) and the **Vegetarian Society's** SCREAM Campaign specialise in the protection of animals, especially those that are eaten or used for experiments.

Educational groups

Some groups specialise in education, like the **World Wide Fund for Nature (WWF)**. They receive charitable grants and are able to supply schoolteachers and pupils with information about wildlife, environment and forests, for example. You can usually get an information pack free.

Recreational conservationists

The **Ramblers**, birdwatchers, climbers and hillwalkers are all considered to be recreational conservationists. They regard the beauty of the planet as a source of pleasure but don't always get involved with pressure groups or campaigning. They are often good at first-hand conservation practices, like protecting the places they visit.

Deep Ecology is a spiritual movement. It is called 'deep' ecology because it encourages people to think more deeply about the planet, accepting and agreeing that they are actually part of it and part of the history of the cycles affecting the earth. The Deep Ecology movement offers workshops called the Council of All Beings. In these, people learn to accept themselves as part of nature. They can openly show grief for the dying planet and can learn more about the power that nature holds to heal itself and the human population.

Habitat

A habitat is not a furniture shop, it is a place where a plant grows or an animal feeds and breeds – each habitat is the home of that species, and if the habitat is destroyed, the species, too, will often die.

About 1,100 sq km of natural habitat are razed, paved, chopped down, dredged up or poisoned around the world *every day*. The land gained from cutting down habitat is used by human beings for various things – AGRICULTURE, raising animals for MEAT, building houses and making roads.

The first threat these developments pose is to the wildlife which lives on the land. Plants and animals alike are threatened, and we create many ENDANGERED SPECIES this way.

Then there is the depletion of the land once it has been developed. In the case of the RAINFORESTS, once the habitat has been destroyed the land is practically worthless after a few years. Elsewhere, rich natural life systems are destroyed, and poorer life systems replace them (as in the case of excessive planting of conifer FORESTS in Britain). SOIL is also depleted and lost.

Destruction of habitat has wider implications as well – it contributes to the GREENHOUSE EFFECT and the spread of DESERTS. By destroying natural habitat we are not only harming the balance of nature, we are storing up disasters for the future.

■ *What can you do?*

Encourage your school, college or local library to mount an exhibition on local habitats, or do a project yourself on the subject.

Find out how you can work directly to help save natural habitat. The British Trust for Conservation Volunteers, the National Trust, the Field Studies Council and Friends of the Earth are all good places to begin. Some of these organisations run holidays where you can work on the land, putting back a little of what has been taken out.

Hamburgers

Here's a sample recipe for a quarter-pound beefburger:

    30 g beef shin (including gristle, sinew and some fat)
    16 g beef mince (including heart, tongue and more fat)
    19 g rusk and soyaflour
    16 g chopped beef fat
    20 g water
     2 g salt and spices
     1 g monosodium glutamate and colouring
    0.5 g polyphosphates and preservative
    10 g MRM (mechanically recovered meat – partly fat)

Grind the beef, add the mince, rusk and soyaflour, fat, water, flavourings, colourings and preservatives. (The last three are ADDITIVES.) Then add the MRM. Shape, cook, put in a bun and eat.

Do you fancy ordering that? Doesn't sound appetising, does it? Particularly when you realise that mechanically recovered MEAT is produced by machines which 'tumble-massage' stripped animal carcasses to get the last shreds of tissue off. The resulting 'meat' is finely chopped and ground by machine and then bound with emulsifiers and thickeners to stop the whole ugly mass falling apart. Hamburger meat can also legally include offal – lungs, stomach and testicles, for example.

Polyphosphate salts have the effect of holding and absorbing water into meat, so they add weight without ingredients. Monosodium glutamate is a chemical meat tenderiser.

And look at the high proportion of fat! Even though the hamburger contains some protein, you have to eat your way through a lot of animal fat to get to it.

■ *What can you do?*

Eat bean burgers (but ask if they've been cooked in beef fat).

Write to your favourite hamburger manufacturer and ask them to supply a list of the ingredients in their burgers, which may vary from the 'typical' burger described above. Then you'll know exactly what you're eating! See also FAST FOOD.

Hazardous Waste

Hazardous (or toxic) waste is the poisonous by-product of our industries and our lifestyles. It contains a mixture of various CHEMICALS which need to be disposed of. Because it is so poisonous, it is very difficult to find a way of getting rid of it safely.

We generate a good deal of hazardous waste. In 1984 Britain created about 4 million tonnes of it; in the same year, the USA generated about 260 million tonnes, or one tonne per person.

Hazardous waste has up till now generally been dumped in LANDFILL SITES, in the SEAS or pressed into deep wells. This has created pollution, and a number of clean-up operations will need to take place to make the waste safe once more. Finding places to dump hazardous waste is a problem, too; nobody wants it on their doorstep.

A new and sinister way of dumping hazardous waste is emerging. Sites for disposal of hazardous waste in Europe are becoming scarce. So hazardous waste is sometimes taken to developing countries, who are paid to dispose of it, and often do so with little regard for safety. This could lead to pollution problems for the developing countries, who are already under environmental and economic pressure.

There is no safe way of disposing of hazardous waste. We must drastically reduce the amount created in the first place.

■ *What can you do?*

Read the sections on WASTE and HEAVY METALS for some ideas on how to cut down your own contribution to hazardous waste.

Heavy Metals

Heavy metals have nothing to do with rock music. They are the metals from the chemical table of elements which are dense, metallic and weigh a lot.

Some of these metals are essential 'trace elements' for our bodies. Manganese, copper and zinc are needed by humans in tiny quantities to function properly, though in larger quantities they become a health hazard. Other heavy metals, which are used in industrial processes and may be contained in everyday household objects, also pose dangers.

Certain heavy metals, like LEAD, mercury and cadmium, are poisonous. Chemical compounds of these elements can build up in animals, plants and human bodies. Lead, for example, poisons the nervous system. The metals cannot be destroyed, only changed from one compound to another.

Poisonous heavy metals can get into our bodies in a number of ways. When heavy metals are used in industrial processes, they are taken from stable deposits in the earth. This causes pollution near the mines. The metals are processed in a factory, and particles escape in the smoke and water.

Once a product containing heavy metals has been used, it has to be disposed of, and this causes even greater environmental pollution. Some countries, like Sweden, restrict the use of certain metals for this reason.

You can find environmentally harmful heavy metals in PLASTIC, BATTERIES and dental fillings.

■ *What can you do?*

Look after your teeth. Mercury is used in amalgam dental fillings.

Avoid nickel-cadmium batteries unless they are the rechargeable type, and always dispose of them carefully.

Brightly coloured plastics used for household objects like

washing-up bowls can contain cadmium. You are probably better off buying light-coloured plastics.

Avoid lead, both in petrol and in paint.

Hormones

Hormones are vital in the human body. They are chemical substances transported in the blood to trigger specific effects. Some farm animals are given injections of synthetic hormones to make them more productive.

In the United States, an oestrogen-based hormone known as DES used to be implanted into beef, cattle and sheep to make them grow faster. It was shown to cause cancer and was withdrawn, but other hormones which may have the same effect are still available.

In Britain, too, there is controversy over a hormone known as BST, which makes a dairy cow produce nearly 20 per cent more milk. The hormone is being tested on some UK farms, and there is no way of knowing whether the milk you are drinking has been BST-treated.

In some countries, it is not just meat and milk that are risky. In the past few years, an epidemic of 'thelarche' has occurred in Puerto Rico. Thelarche is premature sexual development, shown in early breast enlargement, development of pubic hair and menstruation in children as young as 18 months. The epidemic was thought to be caused by chicken farmers using hormones to fatten their poultry more quickly.

■ *What can you do?*

Consider going VEGETARIAN, at least until you can be sure about the hormone content of the meat you buy.

Write to your supermarket manager and ask if your supermarket buys meat from suppliers who use hormones.

Contact your milk company and ask if they are supplying milk from BST-treated cows. The organisation Compassion in World Farming have a good resource pack on BST.

Irradiation

Irradiation is the zapping of fresh food with RADIATION to help make it last longer. Environment and health groups insist that it is unnecessary and potentially dangerous.

Irradiation factories use cobalt-60 or caesium-137, which emit gamma rays, to irradiate the food. This kills bacteria and delays the ageing of food. However, irradiation has been found to reduce the vitamin content of food and affects its balance of essential fatty acids. The long-term effects of food irradiation are as yet unknown. Environmental groups claim that the process is simply a way of using up nuclear waste and making nuclear radiation more acceptable to the public.

By 1989 no standard symbol had been introduced to show that food has been irradiated, and currently there is no reliable test to check if it has been. No legislation had been passed to safeguard workers at potential food-irradiation plants.

■ *What can you do?*

Ask whether any food you suspect – it is most likely to be vegetables or fruit – has been irradiated. Write to the London Food Commission for more information.

Support supermarkets who say they won't stock irradiated food. What's your local supermarket's policy?

Write to the Department of Health and the Department of the Environment.

Jewellery

Some of our most beautiful and exotic jewellery comes directly from animals or the seas. Until very recently turtle shells, which are found in the waters round the equator, were used for bracelets and charms.

It is now illegal to buy or sell any product from some turtles, like the hawksbill turtle, because they are an ENDANGERED SPECIES. ELEPHANTS have been killed for ivory for jewellery and their skins have been used for watch straps and handbags.

Coral reefs, which support one-third of all the fish species in the oceans, are also endangered. Although overfishing and waste dumping are the primary concerns, collecting coral for jewellery and trinkets also causes damage.

■ What can you do?

Don't buy coral jewellery and refuse to buy exotic shell and coral souvenirs.

Don't buy ivory, animal skins or other exotic or endangered animal trinkets.

You might want to join the Environmental Investigation Agency which exposes trades in animals, or the World Wide Fund for Nature who campaign and educate around the world.

Keeping sane

(Or Green Humour is in . . .)

Environmentalists have a difficult job. After all, being the Green Superwoman and Superman, saving the planet from death and destruction and generally cleaning up the mess that's gone on for the past few decades is a serious and difficult task.

But if you can't laugh, it won't work. Humour is one of the most important ingredients for saving the planet. If we are too serious no one is going to listen to us, and eventually people are going to turn off.

A really good reason to be happy is that you'll find that more people will join you and be on your side – who wants to join the 'Oh we're all going to die and it's terrible' party?

Try introducing humour in all your actions, thoughts and feelings about the environment and you'll probably end up lasting longer and keeping sane!

■ What can you do?

Try thinking of as many really silly campaigns as you can.

Have a 'We're Saving the Planet Party'.

Write limericks about the environment – they are easy and soon get people smiling.

Have fun yourself. If it really is getting heavy, think about why you're doing it and if you want to carry on. You might need a break and go back to it later on in order to keep really sane.

Landfill Sites

Landfill sites are used for waste disposal for most of the world's HAZARDOUS and domestic WASTE.

A landfill site at its most basic is a large hole in the ground into which a mixture of WASTE is tipped and left to decompose. Modern 'sanitary' landfills tip it into specially prepared cells and cover it daily. Because of the mixture of wastes in our dustbins, household waste is more hazardous than you think. Plastics, batteries, inks, heavy metals etc, all mix together to create a potential time bomb.

In 1989, British government ministers voiced serious concern about the 1,400 landfill sites in Britain that are posing a variety of problems. Methane gas emissions have already caused serious problems including explosions, even though the gas could be harnessed as an alternative source of energy. And rotting waste, mixed with rainwater, seeps through the ground. This noxious mixture can be up to 1000 times stronger that domestic sewage.

To try to solve the problem of leakage, some countries have limited the landfilling of hazardous waste to sites which are lined with clay or plastic to prevent the materials seeping into underlying soil. But the sites can overflow if it rains heavily, and recent research suggests that any lining will leak eventually. The USA decided to phase out all landfilling of hazardous waste by 1990. Britain, however, continues to maintain that landfilling is a safe option.

A large number of landfill sites are necessary to cope with all the waste we generate, and it is difficult to find suitable places to put them. In fact, it is estimated that Britain will run out of possible sites by the year 2000.

■ *What can you do?*

You can help reduce the pressure to build landfill sites by generating less waste. See the suggestions under WASTE, RECYCLING and PACKAGING

Never let children play on currently used landfill sites. Take notice of the warning signs, and avoid the sites yourself too.

Lead

Lead is a HEAVY METAL which exists naturally and is used in a number of commercial products. Lead can be found in most paint and varnishes, in primers, in petrol, BATTERIES, some toys and some cosmetics.

Other sources of lead include DRINKING WATER from old lead-lined water tanks and plumbing, and AIR POLLUTION from CARS and factories.

Lead is a poison. (It is thought that the Romans suffered badly from drinking out of lead cups, and that people in the seventeenth century died from using lead-based cosmetics on their skins.) It can be ingested or inhaled. Symptoms of lead poisoning include stomach pains, irritability and headaches. Lead is poisonous to animals, too: swans have died because of lead they have swallowed from weights used on fishing rods. The use of lead in petrol can produce DIOXINS.

Perhaps most importantly, lead causes damage to children's brains. It can also damage unborn children.

■ *What can you do?*

Avoid sources of lead whenever possible. Read the label on paint cans before you buy.

Get a briefing about lead from the National Society for Clean Air.

Don't use lead weights, which are now in any case prohibited, when fishing.

Encourage your family to go lead-free with your car.

Malnutrition

Malnutrition is the result of not getting enough food or eating a very poor diet for a long period. Half the world's population is going hungry. More than two-thirds of these people live in Asia, and most of the rest in Africa and Latin America.

In theory, world AGRICULTURE should be able to produce enough food for the whole planet, but resources are being mismanaged. The CASH CROP system and misguided projects in the developing world have all helped create the conditions for starvation in the midst of plenty. Overproduction of MEAT means that valuable grain which could feed people is being fed to cattle. Meanwhile 30,000 children die in the developing world *every day* from malnutrition-related disease.

■ *What can you do?*

Often you can find out about world hunger just by reading the newspapers. Get more information from the aid agencies listed in the back of the book.

Try cutting out sweets for a week and send the money you have saved to one of the aid agencies.

See also the suggestions under CASH CROPS and MEAT.

Meat

Meat is not cheap. It costs the lives of millions of animals and is helping to endanger our environment.

Over half the world's cereal harvest is fed to animals reared for slaughter. If that grain was used to feed humans instead, we could take a huge step towards dealing with world starvation (see MALNUTRITION). We could avoid what happened during the Ethiopian famine of 1984–5, when grain from starving Ethiopia was imported to Britain and other countries to feed cattle.

Cutting down our meat consumption could save land by preserving the RAINFORESTS which are destroyed to ranch cattle. It is estimated that 9 sq metres of rainforest are lost for every HAMBURGER produced this way. Cutting down on meat would also cut down on the methane belched out by cattle, which contributes to the GREENHOUSE EFFECT. Eating less meat could keep us healthier by reducing our fat and HORMONE intake. We would not be supporting the cruel techniques of FACTORY FARMING either.

■ *What can you do?*

Try to cut down on the meat in your diet. Contact the Vegetarian Society who can offer a lot of ideas and support.

Spread the word. Many people are unaware of the real implications of eating meat. If everyone were to cut down or complain, things would have to change. The meat industry might even think again about its methods of operation.

Organise a vegetarian event of some kind, and send the profits to one of the international aid organisations or to a rainforest charity – to put back some of what is being taken out!

Noise

Don't cringe, don't switch off. There is a form of pollution that surrounds you every day, yet you may not be aware of the damage it is doing you because it is very rarely called pollution. It is just called noise.

Whether you live in a city or not, your environment is much noisier today than it was in the early years of the century. Traffic, machinery and aeroplanes all contribute to a higher overall sound level, while in the city, street repairs, construction sites, loud music, trains and CARS all add to the din.

Loud sounds destroy sensory cells in the inner ear, and these do not regenerate. Continuous exposure to loud noise has made us expect to go deaf as we get older. Yet this is unnecessary. West Africans in their seventies have better hearing than Londoners in their twenties.

People who live near motorways and airports have been found to visit their doctors more often. They have more stress-related illnesses and more psychological problems. Other signs of stress – disturbed sleep, high blood pressure, ulcers and headaches – can also be attributed indirectly to noise in the environment.

It is frustrating and disturbing to be exposed to high levels of noise. One researcher suggests that the noise from a single motorbike after midnight in a large city can wake up thousands of people. Loud parties, personal stereos and having the volume up too high on the television can disturb people around you.

■ *What can you do?*

Be aware of the noise you and others create. Is it necessary?

Try to avoid extremely loud noise. Don't stand too near the loudspeakers at pop concerts, and, if you want to, use earplugs.

Negotiate a 'noise agreement' with the people who live around you. If they want to play music late at night but you have to get up early, see if you can come to an arrangement that they only make a lot of noise at weekends, when you can sleep in – and vice versa!

If you are suffering from continuous loud noise, get in touch with the Noise Abatement Society, who have a number of suggestions as to how to deal with it. They also campaign against noise generally.

You can phone your local council or the police to complain about loud and persistent noise in your area.

Nuclear Power

Nuclear power provides around 3 per cent of the world's commercial energy. About thirty years ago, when the nuclear-power industry began, some scientists claimed that the electricity produced would be virtually free. Instead, this form of energy is costing us a great deal of money and creating a wide range of environmental, social and political problems. It is a highly controversial issue.

Nuclear power is generated from the naturally radioactive element uranium (see RADIATION). The uranium is mined in Australia, southern Africa, the USA and Canada. In many mines in southern Africa, workers lack health and safety facilities and many miners get lung cancer. The mines pollute the environment with radioactive radon gas. Mines in Canada have badly polluted ten different lakes.

The uranium is shipped to countries around the world who use it to fuel their nuclear power stations. The fuel operates like a very slow and controlled nuclear bomb, generating vast amounts of heat which is used to produce steam and the steam is used to produce electricity.

Radioactive leaks and accidents sometimes occur. Examples

are CHERNOBYL in Russia in 1986 and Three Mile Island in Pennsylvania, in the United States, in 1979, where the radio-active core of a power station melted down. So far, it has cost $1,000 million to clean up. The United States has not built any nuclear power stations for 15 years because they are thought to be uneconomic and unsafe.

In Britain, several families are trying to sue the British nuclear industry because their children have died or are dying of leukaemia, a cancer found in clusters around nuclear power stations.

Nuclear power stations produce nuclear waste, which is taken for reprocessing to Sellafield, in Cumbria. There, spent nuclear fuel is treated. But the process, even though it creates some reusable uranium and PLUTONIUM, produces even more nuclear waste than there was in the first place.

Unfortunately, scientists didn't work out what to do with the waste before they built nuclear power stations and now we are left with tonnes of radioactive waste that takes thousands of years to become safe. PLUTONIUM, which is a by-product of reprocessing and used in bombs and fast breeder reactors, will take 24,000 years before it is half as dangerous as it is now.

■ *What can you do?*

Use electricity carefully. Saving electricity means there will be less demand for nuclear power stations to be built. See the section on ENERGY CONSERVATION for more ideas.

Join a local campaign against nuclear power, especially if you have a power station in your area. Write to Friends of the Earth or Greenpeace to find out about local groups.

Write to British Nuclear Fuels Ltd and learn their arguments for the continued use of nuclear power.

Organic

Organic farming uses an ecological, rather than a chemical, approach. It aims to retain the long-term fertility of soil, to avoid all forms of chemical pollution, to reduce the use of energy in AGRICULTURE and to treat all livestock humanely.

Organic farming concentrates on some of the oldest principles of farming. An organic farmer will try to keep the soil fertile by using soil-improving plants like clover and natural FERTILISERS instead of CHEMICALS. Instead of growing just one crop, organic farming rotates crops, growing something different every year for a three- or four-year cycle so that the soil does not become drained of nutrients. Keeping things varied in this way also means that pests find it harder to attack the crops, because the crop keeps changing and they have to adapt.

Mass-produced food, grown intensively with chemicals to make high yields possible, is usually heavily subsidised by government money. The price of organic food reflects what raising a crop actually costs.

Organic food *is* more expensive. But many people say it tastes better than mass-produced food, and if you can buy it, you will be doing something very important. More farmers will realise that there is a demand for organic produce and will think about turning their land over to producing it. What you buy can encourage them to do this – and we hope that, as more farmers go organic, the price will come down.

■ *What can you do?*

Buy organic sometimes, even if you can't buy it every time. See if your supermarket has begun to stock organic produce.

You can get organic fruit, vegetables, bread and sometimes even meat.

Grow your own organic food in your garden (see GARDENING). Join the Soil Association, who encourage and monitor organic growers. Or take a cheap weekend break to grow organic food for someone else on an organic farm. Contact Working Weekends on Organic Farms for details.

Ozone Layer

Above our heads, at a height of between 20 and 50 km, is a thin layer of an oxygen-related gas called ozone. This fragile layer is crucial to our life on the planet. It filters out around 99 per cent of the ultraviolet RADIATION of the sun. Without the ozone layer, this radiation would probably kill most of us.

The world's ozone layer is thinning. Human activities have damaged it to the extent that it has developed periodic tears above the poles.

Scientists estimate that even a 1 per cent reduction in the ozone in the atmosphere could cause 15,000 new cases of skin cancer in the USA alone. It could cause thousands of cataracts and other eye diseases. An increase in ultraviolet radiation could also be a disaster for crops and plant life, and it would threaten the plankton in the seas, the tiny plants and animals on which we depend for much of the oxygen we breathe.

The greatest threat to the ozone layer is posed by chloroflourocarbons – CFCs for short. These gases course through the ozone layer destroying its molecules. They are used in AEROSOLS, refrigerants (used to keep fridges and freezers cold), and many other products. There is conclusive proof that CFCs damage the ozone layer, and international measures are being taken to the limit their production.

■ *What can you do?*

Following the suggestions under CFCs will help protect the ozone layer.

To protect yourself, never sunbathe without a sunscreen – ever.

Wear sunglasses in bright sunshine.

Packaging

If you buy a friend a box of chocolates, you'll probably be paying more for the layers of paper and foil than for the sweets inside. Some 80 per cent of our household WASTE is packaging: PLASTICS, glass, PAPER, cardboard and tins.

Nature has provided its own wrapping for many foods. Oranges, bananas, nuts and vegetables all come in their own packages, and yet we waste millions of trees wrapping them up again. It is estimated that we pay £5,000 million every year for packaging in the UK, much of which ends up being dumped in our overloaded LANDFILL SITES.

Packaging also allows food to be stacked efficiently on shelves, and labelling can give us information about the product. But it would be much better if all packaging were efficient, recyclable (see RECYCLING) and BIODEGRADABLE.

Unfortunately, it usually isn't. A case in point is the plastic bags we take away in their millions from shops and supermarkets. The vast majority of these cause long-term problems in the environment. They are now banned in some supermarkets in Italy.

■ *What can you do?*

Try to avoid overpackaged goods when shopping. One layer of packaging – like a bag – should be ample. Choose paper bags over plastic ones.

Refuse plastic carrier bags. Take your own shopping bag or basket instead.

Try to avoid packaging which is made of mixed materials, like plastic-backed paper or foil-backed plastic. This makes the packaging impossible to recycle.

Try to recycle BOTTLES and CANS.

Buy refillable containers when you can – the Body Shop refills its bottles. This saves money, too!

Buy things in large quantities if you have room to store them. Bulk buying means less packaging.

Paper

In Britain alone, 7.7 million tonnes of paper is used every year, and 5.5 million tonnes of this is thrown away, ending up in LANDFILL SITES. By throwing away paper, we are helping to destroy the world's FORESTS and RAINFORESTS and threatening the balance of life on the planet.

Whole forests have been planted just to meet our paper demands. Native British and European forests are being replaced by thousands of acres of conifer plantations. These 'artificial forests' are often planted in soil that is not meant for this type of tree, and the trees are literally forced to grow. This leads to a loss of SOIL nutrients, plants, HABITAT and wildlife in the area.

Rainforests in Central America and Asia are being cut down and replaced with eucalyptus trees to be used for paper production. The eucalyptuses soak up so much water from the soil that they affect the delicate water balance. This causes devastating soil erosion and environmental damage.

Because trees soak up carbon dioxide, we are increasing the quantity of carbon dioxide in the air when we cut trees down. Carbon dioxide is one of the gases responsible for the GREEN-HOUSE EFFECT, so overuse of paper and wood products means we are contributing to that, too.

We also contribute to the Greenhouse Effect by the process of paper production from wood pulp. Energy is needed to drive the mills that produce paper, and using that energy, if it comes from FOSSIL FUELS, adds to the levels of carbon dioxide in the air. If the paper is bleached with CHLORINE, the paper mills add the environmental hazard of poisonous DIOXINS.

We must make better use of our paper. We can reuse paper

products instead of using them once and throwing them away, or we can recycle them. By RECYCLING paper, we can save up to 50 per cent of the energy needed for paper production while at the same time reducing the amount of WASTE we produce.

Recycling paper is a fairly straightforward process, and it is something we should all support. It can really make a difference. If the world were to recycle half its paper, 40,000 km of land could be saved from being used to grow trees for paper. And by helping preserve the forests, we can help preserve the planet.

◼ *What can you do?*

Reuse all the paper you can. Use the backs of envelopes for shopping lists and paper bags from fruit shops for taking sandwiches to school. Give old cereal boxes to your local playgroup so that they can use the cardboard for making models.

If you cut envelopes open carefully, you can use them again. You can buy labels for resealing them from environmental organisations and charities. Many labels carry a 'save the trees' message.

Use recycled writing paper and toilet paper, which you can buy at many stationers and supermarkets. Urge any groups you work with to use recycled paper, too.

Try to avoid buying paper you don't really need. Complain when you get too many layers of PACKAGING, for example with FAST FOOD.

Look for renewable alternatives to paper products, like cotton handkerchiefs instead of DISPOSABLE tissues.

If you can't use paper again, don't just throw it away! Find a paper merchant or phone Friends of the Earth or your local council to see if they will take your old newspapers.

You may want to set up a local paper-collection scheme to raise money and awareness. Ask your school or college to set up a waste-paper collection point, and encourage people to collect and reuse their paper.

Pesticides

Pesticides are CHEMICALS designed to kill spiders, worms, flies, rodents and other small animals and insects. They are sprayed over crops and trees. In the United Kingdom in 1988, 26 million kg of pure pesticides were sprayed on our food. In the United States, the annual figure is a staggering 2.6 billion tonnes.

Pesticides don't kill just the animals or insects they are supposed to. They also kill other mammals like field mice who feed off insects, and in turn affect birds who eat the mice. Pesticide residues seep into waterways, affecting ground water, fish and even DRINKING WATER.

Many of the chemicals sprayed on our food can cause cancers or have other long-term effects. Human breast milk worldwide contains pesticide residues, and the World Health Organisation is seriously concerned that this will affect the health of our next generation.

Lax standards mean that pesticides that are banned in the United States and other developed countries can be produced and sold to developing countries. Dieldrin, once used on potatoes in the UK, is a good example. Since the early 1980s it has been banned in the developed countries, but a multinational company still produces it and sends it to countries like the Philippines.

The companies who produce pesticides claim that the world would not be able to feed itself unless pests were killed with their products. But many studies disagree. British government officials found in the 1980s that by reducing pesticides in AGRICULTURE, crops actually increased over a period of time, rather than the other way around. The difficulty is how to get world agriculture off the pesticides it is now dependent on using.

▊ *What can you do?*

Always wash fresh fruit and vegetables carefully. Many pesticide residues can be removed this way.

Be careful about feeding food treated with pesticides to babies. The chemicals used can be particularly dangerous for them.

Buy ORGANIC food whenever you can.

Support campaigns run by environmental groups for clear, effective labelling of fresh fruit and vegetables so you can know exactly what you are eating.

See also ALLERGIES, CASH CROPS, COTTON, DDT.

Pets

In the United States and Canada, pet dogs and cats eat more MEAT than the entire human population of South America. In Britain, pets eat 651,000 tonnes of meat every year. The meat that ends up in pet foods usually comes from developing countries. Some tuna fished for cat food contributes indirectly to the killing of DOLPHINS.

Many pets are fed on tinned food. This uses up to 2 billion tins, and the food is contaminated with LEAD and contains chemical ADDITIVES, sugar, artificial flavourings and salt. This is bad for the pets, who become addicted to them.

Pets affect the environment in other ways, too. In Britain every year 1,000 million tonnes of dog faeces and over 4.5 million litres of urine foul up public streets and pavements. Children have gone blind from contact with dog faeces. In some areas, worms and small reptiles are disappearing because so many cats are eating them.

Some animals that are bought as pets, like parrots and exotic birds, are ENDANGERED SPECIES, and when they are brought from the wild, it diminishes the already small populations. Unwanted pets are a problem, too: 1,000 unwanted dogs are put down every year in Britain.

Many pets offer companionship and dogs may make you feel secure, but if you want a pet, you should be prepared to look after it well and in an ecological way.

■ *What can you do?*

If you are considering buying a pet, think hard about why you want it. Can your needs be met by other means?

Don't buy endangered species caught in the wild, like parrots and exotic birds.

Read the tips from the Royal Society for the Protection of Cruelty to Animals (RSPCA) and, if you have a dog, the League for the Introduction of Canine Control on caring for pets. Train your dog properly.

Try your dog on VEGETARIAN food. (Cats must eat meat to survive.) Ask the Vegetarian Society for details of a healthy diet for your dog. Cats and dogs should really be eating raw food, but if you want your pet to change, it may take a while to wean it off processed food.

Plastics

Plastic in its many forms has become one of the world's most common substances. A comparatively new and cheap by-product of the petroleum industry, it has replaced paper, wood, metal and many other types of material.

The big problem with plastic is that it is not BIODEGRADABLE. This means that when you throw it away it does not break down completely in the soil into an inert and 'environment-friendly' substance as, for example, paper does. And when plastic is burned, it produces DIOXINS.

Some plastics can be recycled, but only into plastic bags to put more rubbish into. Even then, the technology is unable to separate different types of plastic effectively. Some companies claim that they have made a biodegradable or photo-degradable plastic (one that breaks down in light), but the British Plastics Federation assert that none of these substances is truly biodegradable and that the plastic only breaks down into pieces small enough to be invisible to the human eye.

Some plastics are actually dangerous. Throw-away plastic clingfilm used for food wrapping may contain plasticisers or vinyl chloride. These are poisonous chemicals which can get into food, especially if the food is warm or fatty. Hard plastics, like kitchen dustbins, can contain cadmium, which is a HEAVY METAL.

■ What can you do?

Reuse plastic whenever you can. Plastic margarine containers and yoghurt tubs are a good alternative to wrapping food in cling film. They make quite useful flower pots (see GARDENING) and storage pots, too.

Don't accept plastic carrier bags. Take a canvas shopping bag with you when you go out, or a basket. If you have a stock of plastic carriers, they make very good pedal-bin liners, and save you buying new plastic bin liners.

Say 'no' to overwrapped foodstuffs (see also PACKAGING).

Don't buy brightly coloured plastics unless you can be sure they don't contain cadmium.

Plutonium

Plutonium is generally regarded as one of the most dangerous elements ever created. A small amount, the size of an orange, could completely obliterate a city if it exploded. It takes only a tiny amount of plutonium to make a nuclear bomb, and it is officially admitted that even a tiny speck of it, too small for the human eye to see, could cause cancer (SEE RADIATION).

Plutonium is artificially created in nuclear reactors by bombarding uranium-238 with neutrons. The uranium absorbs a neutron and changes into plutonium. Plutonium is extracted by reprocessing nuclear waste for use in an advanced type of reactor called a fast breeder and in nuclear bombs. Fast-breeder reactors are both expensive and difficult to operate.

Plutonium lasts for a very long time. It has a half-life of 24,000 years. A half-life is the amount of time needed for the element to decompose to only half its radioactive level. In other words, the plutonium in the world today looks as though it will last practically for ever.

Countries with nuclear reprocessing plants, such as Britain and France, have built up large stocks of plutonium. In Britain, some 35 tonnes of plutonium are kept under strict security at Sellafield, in Cumbria.

■ *What can you do?*

Write to British Nuclear Fuels Ltd asking them to explain their arguments in favour of reprocessing and using plutonium.

If you are against the making of plutonium and its use in nuclear weapons, join an organisation like the Campaign for Nuclear Disarmament (CND), whose first priority is stopping the world production and use of nuclear weapons.

Write to your Member of Parliament and ask if any plutonium is stockpiled in your area. You aren't officially allowed to know but you can use this as a good way of voicing your concern.

Preservatives

Salting, smoking, wind-drying and pickling have been used for years to make sure that food lasts. Today we have more methods of preservation, but we cannot be totally sure that they are all safe.

Canning and bottling are both fairly safe preserving methods, although the cans and glass need to be properly disposed of (see BOTTLES, CANS). Freezing and drying are also reasonably safe, but frozen food needs huge amounts of energy to keep it frozen, and most fridges and freezers use CFCs.

Food can also be preserved by using CHEMICALS, and this is another matter. Like many ADDITIVES, some chemical preservatives are thought to be dangerous or at least dubious. Of the 45 most common preservatives, 29 have been found to cause side effects including skin irritations, asthma, nausea, vomiting, stomach problems and destruction of red blood cells.

Of the preservatives that accumulate in the body it is difficult to know exactly how much may be poisonous, but one study in the United States showed that when nitrite consumption was reduced (nitrite is one of the most widespread preserving chemicals), the rate of stomach cancer dropped.

It is probably a good idea to avoid preservatives unless they are known to be safe. Fresh food has few preservatives, though IRRADIATION of fresh food is legal in Britain.

■ *What can you do?*

Buy fresh, natural food when you can. The ideal would be to buy ORGANIC food.

Be aware that even food that contains preservatives can go 'off'. Many cases of food poisoning have been caused by bad storage or inadequate preparation of food.

Public Transport

Apart from CYCLING and walking, public transport is the most efficient way of travelling, for you and for the environment.

Public transport means that people can get around in a way that uses fuel efficiently. If you multiply the distance travelled on a litre of fuel by the number of passengers carried, public transport is much more efficient than private CARS. A car carrying one passenger can travel 9 km on a single litre of petrol. But a bus carrying 50 people can travel 50 km on one litre: 50 km per litre per person.

Like cars, public transport pollutes and needs roads, but it reduces the environmental damage significantly. Fewer cars mean less AIR POLLUTION and a reduced contribution to the GREENHOUSE EFFECT. Travelling by public transport is also cheaper than travelling by car – just ask any car owner how much it costs to keep their vehicle on the road.

In their Cities for People campaign, started in 1986, Friends of the Earth set out the advantages of a good public-transport system. It would reduce noise, congestion, pollution and the number of road accidents. Clearing the roads of too many vehicles would make them safer for cyclists, as well as for ambulances and fire engines. Fewer cars would mean fewer areas of public open land having to have roads built on them. A better transport system would also make life easier and safer for non-drivers.

Some European countries, like France, pride themselves on their excellent train facilities, ranging from crèches to cheaper fares and meals included in the price. In 1988 Britain spent £3,600 million on roads and only £1,400 million on public transport.

Better public-transport facilities for all of us would mean better access for old people, disabled people and women with children. It would mean more attention to the safety of trains and passengers, more late-night services in cities, and other improvements.

Although it may take a while for all of us to get used to the idea of buses and trains rather than cars, the benefits for us and for the environment would be enormous.

■ *What can you do?*

Use public transport whenever you can (unless you'd rather walk or cycle).

Don't vandalise, or sit by and watch people vandalise, buses or trains. This takes them out of action for days and causes even more problems and delays.

Decide what kind of public transport you would like to see, and then ask why we haven't got it. You may want to join Transport 2000, to campaign for transport efficiency.

Questions

Asking questions is a vital aspect of being green.

The more informed we become and the more questions we ask, the more we will be able to use our CONSUMER POWER to encourage manufacturers to give us the products we want to buy. The more questions we ask our local councils, the more we will be able to press them to provide the facilities we need. The more questions we ask our governments, the more we will be able to make them alter their policies so that the whole planet can be saved.

We need to be asking questions all the time. If we read an advertisement for a perfume that claims to make us irresistible, we need to remember to ask: 'How is it produced?' 'Is it animal-tested?' 'Do I really need to buy it?' 'Can I find a better equivalent?' And, 'Is the advert just trying to make me discontented with myself?'

What about experts. Often you will see on television or read in the papers that 'an expert' has said something about the environment. Because 'an expert' has said it, you may be more likely to think that it is true. But experts often disagree about things. Ask yourself if they have an axe to grind. You have to make up your own mind.

Don't be afraid to ask questions. A young woman in Wales was asked by her son what would happen if a nuclear bomb dropped. She realised that she did not know, and started writing letters to everyone who might tell her. She ended up writing to and meeting prime ministers around the world.

Radiation

Radiation is a form of energy transmitted as waves or streams of particles. There are two types of radiation: non-ionising radiation, present in light waves, radio waves and microwaves, and ionising radiation, such as X-RAYS, neutrons, and alpha and beta particles. When radiation from NUCLEAR POWER stations is referred to, we mean ionising radiation.

'Radioactive decay' or 'radioactivity' occurs during the decay of atoms that are naturally unstable. The unstable atoms try to change into atoms of other elements to become more stable, emitting radiation as alpha, beta or gamma rays as they do so. Some elements, like carbon-14, potassium-40 and types of uranium, are naturally radioactive; others, like caesium-137, iodine-131 and PLUTONIUM-239 are artificially produced.

Ionising radiation is a health risk because exposure to it can cause chemical changes in the structure of body tissues. The changes can manifest themselves as cancer, where a cell mutates (becomes different), or as disease and damage in future generations because the body's genes have been affected. Radiation increases the chances of cancer developing later in life, and exposure to it is cumulative – every exposure adds to the dose of radiation already in the body. A lot of exposure to radiation can cause 'radiation sickness', which happened to the fire-fighters at CHERNOBYL who were exposed to a very high dose. Children are particularly vulnerable, and cases of childhood leukaemia have been related to radiation from nuclear power stations and plants.

There are two main types of radiation which affect us. The first, known as 'background radiation', comes from natural sources, mostly from radon gas, which is a decay product of natural uranium. By far our greatest exposure – 87 per cent – is to natural radiation. The granite of Cornwall emits radon gas, but the risk from this can be very much reduced by good ventilation.

The risks of exposure to radiation are hotly disputed. Environmentalists claim that any level of exposure is dangerous, increasing the chances of radiation-related illness later in life. They are particularly concerned that the public may be exposed to radiation from radioactive-waste sites. There are 1,250 licensed sites in the UK.

Friends of the Earth have made recommendations for reducing the dose limit for radiation workers and the public. They also argue that the government should provide funds for corrective building and information for houses that have a high level of naturally occurring radon.

■ *What can you do?*

Radiation is a complicated issue. To find out more, write to Friends of the Earth for their booklet 'What Is Radiation?'

If you live near a nuclear power station, reprocessing station or waste site, you can join an environmental group and work with them to campaign for more safety.

See also TELEVISION, IRRADIATION, VDUS.

Rainforests

It is estimated that the tropical rainforests, which circle the earth's equator covering an area the size of the United States, house up to half of all the living things on the planet. There are 30 million different species of insect alone. Many have never even been identified and named – a single tree can house over one thousand new species. The forest is also a haven for a huge diversity of beautiful and abundant tropical vegetation.

The tropical rainforests are being destroyed at the horrific rate of at least once acre – more than a football pitch – per second.

One of the main causes of tropical deforestation is commercial logging. Giant international companies cut down the trees for woods like mahogany and teak. Britain is one of the main importers of tropical hardwoods: we buy the wood to make products like toilet seats, doors, window frames – even coffins! The logging destroys vast areas and for every ten acres cut only one is replanted. Once the forest has been cut down, local farmers move in to use the SOIL.

In Central America, the forests are often burned to clear land to raise cattle. Two-thirds of the Central American rainforest have been destroyed for cattle ranching. Yet local people eat less MEAT than ever before, because the meat is sold to the USA and Canada. It turns up primarily in HAMBURGERS, hot dogs, TV dinners and pet food (see PETS).

Poor people are also being driven into the rainforests. They make their way there either because there is nowhere else for them to go, or with their government's encouragement because of overdevelopment of the more fertile areas (see CASH CROPS). In an attempt to cultivate the forest soil, which is naturally poor and barren once the trees have been cut down, they are forced to resort to cutting and burning which further destroys the land, while native peoples, who have lived in the forests for generations, are driven out.

The burning of the forests releases carbon dioxide, the main gas responsible for the GREENHOUSE EFFECT, into the air. Because trees themselves soak up carbon dioxide, the burning is doubly damaging, removing a natural resource for soaking up the gas while at the same time releasing even more of it. When the trees are removed, the natural balance of the soil is affected, and it dries up, eventually becoming completely useless. Burning down the forests also affects the rainfall patterns and can contribute to both flood and drought, disrupting both the local and the global climate.

The forests contain many plants that are vital to our health. The rose periwinkle, which only grows in the rainforests, contains a natural drug which fights leukaemia (a type of cancer). Scientists believe that the rainforests contain a 'medicine cabinet' of natural drugs which still need to be researched, but the plants that contain them are being irretrievably lost as we destroy their HABITATS. Animals are becoming ENDANGERED

SPECIES or even extinct. The destruction of the rainforests is losing the world one species a day.

The rainforests are now being destroyed at such a rate that only international co-operation can really stop the destruction. But there are also many things that individuals can do to help to halt the process.

■ *What can you do?*

Encourage your family not to buy tropical hardwoods. Read the Friends of the Earth 'Good Wood Guide' before your family buys furniture. It has details of suppliers of timber that has been cut from forests which are being replanted with the same kind of trees. It also has a list of which woods to avoid.

Buy Brazil nuts. These are harvested in the wild and are signs of a healthy rainforest area.

Sign petitions and join campaigns to save the rainforests, such as the one run by Earth Action at Friends of the Earth. Most of the main environmental groups (see the list at the end of the book) are running campaigns to help save the forests.

Support groups like Sting's Forest Action Group and the Rainforest Action Group in Australia, who work specifically to preserve rainforests all over the world, or the Gaia Foundation and Survival International who work for the rights of threatened tribal peoples.

Recycling

Recycling means putting waste back into use. Reuse of a product – for example, using a plastic container that has held ice cream to store salad – is the most direct way of recycling, but products like BOTTLES, CANS, PAPER, metals and textiles can be recycled as raw materials for manufacture of new goods.

Recycling leads to a reduction in the environmental damage caused by the production of goods. It also means there is less WASTE to get rid of (see LANDFILL SITES). It can lead to job creation in collection schemes, recycling workshops and stores of material to be sold for reuse.

Recycling is economic. If Britain were to increase its use of recycled paper, £400 million a year could be saved on importing woodpulp and paper products.

Natural resources all over the world are under pressure. Our industries and the waste we produce are causing terrible pollution. Recycling is a logical way to reduce the damage to our environment and it has the added bonus of saving us money. We must start recycling now!

■ *What can you do?*

There's a lot you can do in this area. Be inventive. How many things do you throw away that could be reused? You could start your own recycling collection at home, or with a group of friends.

Or give unwanted things, or outgrown clothes, to a charity shop.

Do a project on recycling as part of your schoolwork.

Write to Friends of the Earth for information on setting up recycling schemes.

Avoid 'DISPOSABLE' products if you can.

Ask your local council for details of recycling collection points in your area – bottle, can and paper banks – and what their plans are for introducing more.

Consider buying second-hand clothes from charity shops, rather than getting all new things.

Renewable Energy

Renewable energy is derived from sources that will not run out, like the sun and the wind. The idea of harnessing energy from the natural world is not a new one. For many centuries we took power from wind and water, until the Industrial Revolution in the 18th century began to use FOSSIL FUELS (coal, oil and gas).

All renewable energy comes ultimately from the sun. One thousandth of a millionth of the sun's energy is absorbed by the earth. But this is still enough to produce wind and wave power when the sun causes high and low pressures within the air, geothermal power from stored heat in the rocks deep under the earth and solar power, which comes from trapping the energy of the sun itself.

Good examples of renewable energy in action are solar panels, use of methane gas from the WASTE buried in LANDFILL SITES, wind farms (where modern windmills are powering whole areas in the United States), geothermal heating schemes in Europe and wave buoys in the oceans surrounding Iceland and Japan.

Energy from FOSSIL FUELS looks set to run out. We need to look more carefully and more creatively at renewable energy sources for the future. They will need to be funded and researched so they can be put into action effectively, but once working they will not run out.

■ *What can you do?*

Try to save energy (see ENERGY CONSERVATION). The less energy we use, the less pressure there will be to keep finding new ways of providing it.

Find out about renewable energy. It might appeal to you to do a project on it – perhaps as part of a design or science course.

If you have the opportunity, visit the Centre for Alternative Technology in Wales. They have set up a whole community powered entirely by the sun and wind. They also have organic gardens and are a great example of how renewable energy systems work – and they welcome visitors.

Sanitary Products

In 1989 the Women's Environmental Network (WEN) launched a campaign to publicize the environmental consequences of sanitary towels and tampons. They found that until recently, most sanitary towels have been made from CHLORINE-bleached paper pulp. The process used produces highly dangerous chemicals, including DIOXINS. The chemicals are released into the environment and tiny concentrations stay in the towels themselves.

Plastic strips on the backing of sanitary towels are also a problem. When they are flushed down the toilet, they go through the sewage system into rivers and SEAS. There, they do not harmlessly rot (see BIODEGRADABLE). They remain as litter, spoiling the water and endangering wildlife, which can get caught in them.

Tampons might not be a safe alternative to chlorine-bleached towels. They are made from a mixture of COTTON and rayon. The cotton is grown with the use of PESTICIDES and rayon is made by breaking down wood fibres with chlorine gas, again giving rise to dioxins.

Health effects of tampons include toxic shock syndrome, vaginal ulcerations and dryness. Toxic shock syndrome is a rare but serious disease. Symptoms include a high temperature, headache, vomiting and diarrhoea, a sunburnlike rash and rapid drop in blood pressure, which in some cases can lead to death.

Since the WEN campaign, a number of manufacturers have

produced non-chlorine-bleached sanitary towels. Safer tampons may also be a possibility in the future.

■ *What can you do?*

Use the new sanitary towels made from non-chlorine-bleached pulp.

Choose towels with the least PACKAGING, and try to avoid the ones that use plastic.

Don't flush used sanitary towels down the toilet. Put them in the bin instead.

Try reusable, washable sanitary towels, available from good chemists, instead of paper ones.

If you prefer to use tampons, use those with a low absorbency ('regular' rather than 'super' ones). Try to change them less frequently and use towels at night rather than tampons.

Write to maufacturers demanding tampons made from safe cotton. If you want to, you can boycott their products until you get what you want.

Join the Women's Environmental Network and support their campaign.

Seals

In 1988, newspapers suddenly became full of pictures of dead and dying seals. A 'mystery virus' had attacked the seal populations of the North Sea, the Baltic Sea and the Dutch Waddenzee. Estimates of the number of seals who died vary, but at least 7,000 were recorded dead, and the real figure could be much higher.

Scientists are divided as to what caused the outbreak of the virus, but most agree that pollution was a factor. The pollution of the North Sea seemed to have lowered the seals' resistance to infection.

In the Baltic, there were 100,000 grey seals at the beginning of the century – the number has now dropped to between 1,000 and 2,000. Many of those are sterile and most have intestinal or kidney disorders.

In the late 1970s and early 1980s, Greenpeace exposed the extent and methods of seal-hunting in Canada. Seals were being slaughtered in huge quantities for their beautiful silvery-blue skins. Horrific pictures of seals and seal pups who had been clubbed to death began to appear in the papers. Lobbying and demonstrations all over Europe, many instigated by Greenpeace, helped the figures to drop in 1983, but seal-hunting has continued in some areas despite new legislation: 186,000 Canadian seals died in this way in 1986. The rights and wrongs of the slaughter of seals are complicated – many people in Canada for example have traditionally relied on seal-hunting for survival. But environmentalists are concerned that some types of seal will soon become ENDANGERED SPECIES.

Seals are also dying from culling – systemised hunting to keep the seal population down because they compete with the fishing industry. Overfishing in the areas where they live also deprives them of the food they need to survive.

■ *What can you do?*

Cleaning up the sea is one way of helping to save seals. There are suggestions under SEAS.

Consider doing a project on seals as part of a science course.

Join the Marine Conservation Society, the World Wide Fund for Nature or the Young People's Trust for Endangered Species to help campaign to save seals.

Join Greenpeace and help support their campaign against seal-hunting. The publicity for the virus helped people forget that hunting is responsible for far more deaths than the virus.

Seas

Two-thirds of the world is covered in water – our seas. We are polluting them, filling them with poison and WASTE. In 1987 3.5 million tonnes of waste were dumped in the North Sea alone.

Over 300 million gallons of sewage from our toilets floods into Britain's coastal waters each day. Most of this sewage has not been treated to kill the bacteria it contains. Some of these bacteria can cause viral infections in wildlife and humans.

Treated sewage is called sludge. Sludge is dumped at sea. It contains HEAVY METALS, PESTICIDES, DETERGENTS and petroleum derivatives, and dumping it at sea reduces the sea's oxygen level and increases fish disease.

HAZARDOUS WASTE is also dumped at sea. Radioactive waste finds its way into the sea as well. The Irish Sea is considered to be the most radioactively contaminated in the world, and the North Sea contains an estimated 140,000 different chemical substances.

And rubbish ends up in the sea. Even though international legislation has made it illegal to dump PLASTICS at sea, the plastic waste already in the water will not disintegrate in our lifetimes. Plastics still enter the sea from waste like used sanitary towels (see SANITARY PRODUCTS). Six million tonnes of rubbish – glass, tin, wood and food waste, 'DISPOSABLE' containers, bottles and wire – goes into the waters around Britain a year. Plastics kill 2 million seabirds, 100,000 marine mammals and large numbers of turtles and fish around the world every year. Populations of WHALES, SEALS and DOLPHINS are dropping, and pollution is thought to be one of the major causes.

Dumping at sea affects us too. Fish that have fed on toxic (poisonous) material concentrate those toxins in their flesh and fat. When we eat them, toxins and radioactivity can pass into us. Nearly 40 per cent of Britain's litter-strewn beaches fail to meet basic European safety standards. Polluted seawater can poison us, giving us ear and eye infections, hepatitis, even polio or typhoid.

The seas are also being plundered. Coral and shells are taken from their natural HABITAT to provide souvenirs for tourists.

■ *What can you do?*

By creating less waste yourself, you will indirectly help to ensure that less gets dumped at sea. Especially, take all your litter home with you when you visit a beach.

Refuse to buy coral or shells (see JEWELLERY).

Join an organisation fighting to save the seas, like the Marine Conservation Society. Ask for their 'Saving *Your* Seas' pack. Or contact Seas at Risk or Greenpeace for more information.

Contact Friends of the Earth and Greenpeace to find out more about the dumping of waste in the North Sea and what you can do about it.

Soil

The surface of our planet is disappearing. Its soil (earth) is being eroded at the rate of 75 billion tonnes per year. DESERTS are spreading, and remaining soil is being polluted by chemical FERTILISERS and having its minerals washed away.

Overploughing soil, and continually using the same soil to grow the same crop, uses up all its nutrients (see AGRICULTURE). If that goodness is not replaced, the top layer of soil becomes fragile, and can be easily washed or blown away. Generally, this happens too fast for new soil (which is continually being created from weathered rock) to replace what is lost.

Soil all over the world is becoming saltier, and too much salt in soil makes it poisonous to plants. Huge areas of land are becoming too salty (salinised), mainly through irrigation (artifical watering schemes). Figures suggest that, for example, 60–80 per cent of agricultural land in the USSR is already salinised. In countries such as India and Iraq, which could normally be quite productive, salinisation is a growing problem.

Soil erosion can also happen as a result of overstocking land with animals (see MEAT). If too many animals are kept on a piece of land, their grazing can destroy the plant cover which holds the soil together, and the soil can blow away. Natural HABITATS are destroyed. This is particularly happening in areas where once RAINFORESTS grew.

Cutting down FORESTS is always a danger to soil. Often, the roots of trees hold the soil together, and when the trees disappear, the soil tends to disappear too.

■ *What can you do?*

If you can, buy ORGANIC food, which is grown in a way that helps to preserve soil.

Write to the Soil Association for advice on how to look after the soil in your own area.

Join or support campaigns against companies that are cutting down forests and weakening soil cover.

Television

TV is part of our lives, but there are worries that too much television might not be good for us.

Concern about the subtle effects of the low-level electromagnetic RADIATION which is given off by television screens is widespread in some countries, like Sweden. Small children can be affected if they sit very close to the screen. Special low-radiation televisions are now being manufactured which reduce the amounts of radiation given off.

The energy our television sets use is also a problem. In Britain alone, we create 7 million tonnes of carbon dioxide, 10,000 tonnes of sulphur dioxide, 18,500 tonnes of nitrogen oxides and 23.5 cubic metres of nuclear waste from the electricity we use to watch television each year. The gases contribute directly to the GREENHOUSE EFFECT.

Another problem is posed by remote-control television sets. Often they can be turned off only with the remote control. This means they have a little 'on' light which is using up electricity 24 hours a day. Imagine contributing to television-related pollution even while *not* watching TV!

■ *What can you do?*

Try not to watch television for excessively long periods. Think of something else you can do instead.

Don't sit too close to the screen – sit at least two metres away.

Turn the television off if you're not watching it, and if you are, look out for the programmes on the environment.

Suggest that you and your friends watch TV together. This saves energy!

VDUs

The initials VDU stand for 'visual display unit' and refer to the screen of a word processor or computer. A number of surveys have been conducted to see if VDU work is harmful to operators and the results are disturbing.

VDU screens emit low-level RADIATION. If you switch off a VDU in a dark room, you can see a fluorescent glow which remains for some time after the screen has been switched off.

VDUs also emit what are known as 'soft' X-RAYS and, while the machines are designed so that the screen filters them out, old or faulty models let them through.

VDU operators around the world have been found to have many more miscarriages and abnormal births than women who don't use VDUs. This is thought to be caused by the fluctuating electromagnetic field the screens emit. A number of other painful and niggling illnesses have also been associated with VDUs – eyestrain, headaches, blurred vision, skin rashes and itching, and spots.

Strain on the wrists and fingers through too much repetitive typing can lead to diseases like tenosynovitis and tendinitis, where the tendons and the sheaths surrounding the tendons of the arm become painfully inflamed. Bad lighting, which means that operators have to strain towards the screens or fight constant reflections, and badly designed chairs, which put strain on the operators' backs, cause other problems.

It is difficult to ascertain how many of these illnesses are due directly to the VDUs and how many are due to other causes – bad office design, high levels of NOISE, working too many hours and the stress and frustration of having to sit and bang at a keyboard all day. However, there are some precautions which you can take if you have to work for a long time at a computer.

■ What can you do?

If you are working on a computer, take frequent breaks if you can. Once an hour, get up from the desk and walk around, preferably in the fresh air.

Try to make sure that your VDU is set so that light does not reflect off it. A source of light slightly behind you and to your right is best.

Ask your parents or employer for an adjustable desk and chair, so you can adapt them to your own height. The back of the chair should support your whole trunk.

See if you can get a shield or filter for your VDU screen.

Try to be moved away from VDU work if you are, or are trying to become, pregnant.

Vegetarian

'Animals are my friends . . . and I don't eat my friends,' said the playwright, author and vegetarian George Bernard Shaw.

But there are other good reasons why millions of people today have chosen an entirely vegetarian way of life. Vegetarians eat nuts, and all vegetables, eggs and cheese. Some vegetarians eat fish and other cold-blooded animals. Many thousands more have cut back on their consumption of MEAT products.

The first reason is health. The medical profession now thinks that eating too much meat is actually bad for us. Meat requires more energy to digest than many other types of food, and with today's techniques of meat production, there is also the risk of introducing HORMONES and antibiotics to your body. Vegetarians appear to suffer less from heart disease, bowel cancer, gallstones and diabetes because a good, balanced vegetarian diet is a healthy one, high in fibre and low in fat. (Their diet is cheaper than a meat-based one, too.)

Many vegetarians are concerned by the level of cruelty inflicted on animals in the production of our meat (see

FACTORY FARMING). They refuse to eat the food produced by these inhumane and not always clean methods.

Another reason some vegetarians don't eat meat is that they are concerned by the international meat trade and the problems it causes in the developing world. Using grain to feed animals that will be slaughtered often takes away food from people in poor countries. Vast acres of land all over the world have been turned into cattle ranges, including tracts of RAINFOREST.

In Britain 1.3 million children and 1.25 million adults have already become vegetarians. Worldwide there are a growing number of famous vegetarians, too, including Michael Jackson, Madonna and Peter Gabriel.

Veganism is one step on from vegetarianism. It is a way of life which avoids all animal products completely. Vegans will not eat, wear or use any animal-related produce. This means that they eat no meat, fish, eggs, cheese or dairy products: they do not use products like lanolin, which comes from farmed animals, or marine products like WHALE oil. They do not use natural silk, leather or wool.

■ *What can you do?*

If you are not already a vegetarian, consider trying it. Contact the Vegetarian Society, which has a youth section.

Cut down on the meat in your diet, especially red meat like steak and HAMBURGERS, and find other things to replace it. Ask vegetarian friends for advice, or just visit any bookshop or library and see the array of vegetarian cookbooks.

The Vegetarian Society, which operates internationally, has a booklet of ideas for campaigning in and out of school. Ideas include fundraising, animal-welfare workshops and a campaign called Choice! which has been specifically organised to help people campaign for vegetarian meals in schools.

If you are already vegetarian, watch out – meat can be hidden in a lot of places you might not expect it. There can be animal fat in biscuits, gelatine in yoghurts and so on. Read the label of get hold of a listing like the Vegan Society's 'Cruelty Free Shopping'. And watch out for FAST FOOD french fries and 'beanburgers' which may be fried in beef fat!

Waste

This year, you will probably throw out ten times your own body weight in waste.

Textiles, PAPER, glass, PLASTICS, metal, toxic (poisonous) substances and kitchen waste are put out on the doorstep – about 875 kg per person per year in the USA, 680 kg in Australia and 284 kg in Britain. If it stayed on our doorsteps, we would really notice how much waste we are producing!

But the waste doesn't go far away. In Britain, it is usually taken to local dumps, properly called LANDFILL SITES. In some countries, the waste is sorted before it is dumped and the potentially useful parts of it are taken out – BOTTLES, CANS, and PAPER can be recycled, while poisonous substances like cadmium must be disposed of safely. But this doesn't generally happen in Britain: instead, various chemicals in the rubbish begin to react with each other. Inflammable gases are produced, the heavy metals and other toxic substances can be washed into the water supply if it rains, and the whole thing ends up a bulky, poisonous mess.

Waste can be incinerated (burned), and the idea of producing energy from this process seems attractive. But there are problems. If a mixture of waste is burned, toxic gases are produced. Think of the acrid smell that comes from many household bonfires: it comes from burning plastics. If the temperature in the incinerator is not high enough – it needs to be over 900 degrees centigrade – plastics, pesticides and wood preservatives give off DIOXINS, which are more poisonous than cyanide.

These and other poisons remain in the ash, which is then dumped on waste sites. Incinerating mixed rubbish produces more pollutants per unit of energy generated than any other kind of fuel. A better way is to pipe off the gas formed in the waste site. This can produce energy, and the seven schemes in the UK save about 66,000 tonnes of coal a year this way.

Waste is also dumped in the SEAS, polluting them and killing wildlife. Dumping the waste produced by one environment into another is not an answer.

■ *What can you do?*

Sort your own rubbish. The sections on BOTTLES, CANS and PAPER have suggestions on where you can send them for RECYCLING.

If you have a garden you might want to start a compost heap for your kitchen wastes (see under GARDENING).

Once you have got rid of the bottles, cans, paper and kitchen scraps, you can also do something about the plastics (see under PLASTICS for some ideas).

You can cut down on the waste you produce by not buying so much in the first place. Avoid unnecessary PACKAGING and turn down extra bags offered in shops – take your own shopping bag or reuse old carrier bags instead. If you still need bags from shops, paper bags are a better choice than plastic ones, especially if they are made of brown paper, which means they have been recycled.

If you can't find a safe way to dispose of a particular product, send it back to the manufacturers, whose address will be on the packaging, with a letter asking them to dispose of it for you.

Support any schemes in your area which try to clean up waste and litter.

Try not to buy 'DISPOSABLE' things.

Whales

Whales are the largest, and some would say the most beautiful, creatures who grace our seas. They are mammals, rather than fish, and have been found in every one of the earth's oceans and seas. Study of whales has shown that they have a very high intelligence and highly developed social behaviour.

Humans have hunted whales for food and oil since the earliest times, but it was only in the sixteenth century that whales began to be hunted so people could sell their products. Whale oil has been used in lipsticks and creams, leather softeners and machine lubricants. Whalebone stays were used in corsets (not real bone but baleen from the mouth of whales). The commercial whale-hunting industry grew, spreading into the Antarctic, where over 300,000 blue whales were killed in the first half of the twentieth century. By the 1960s, so few blue whales were left in the area that it was not considered worth hunting them any more.

Whale hunting so depleted the population of whales in the world that in 1972 the United Nations called for a moratorium (a short-term ban) on commercial whaling. Action by environmental groups like Greenpeace, who put themselves between whales and whaling ships, helped get the danger to whales into the headlines worldwide. It took ten years to finalise, but in 1982 the International Whaling Commission agreed to a pause in commercial whaling between 1986 and 1990.

But the temporary halt in commercial whaling has not stopped whaling for so-called 'scientific' purposes. Norway and Japan continue killing a smaller number of whales on these grounds, but many people suspect this is an excuse to keep the whaling fleets out on the sea.

Sadly, even this degree of protection may have come too late. It is thought that now there are so few blue whales in the world they cannot find each other to mate, and the blue-whale population has not risen at all since 1965, despite not having been hunted since then. All whales are now badly ENDANGERED SPECIES and some environmentalists fear that in 20 years' time there will be no whales left in the world at all.

■ *What can you do?*

Join the Whale and Dolphin Conservation Society.

Write in protest to the embassies of the countries still whaling – Japan and Norway. (You don't need to know Japanese or Norwegian!)

X-Rays

The biggest source of artificial RADIATION doses to humans is from X-rays.

Where used to make fast diagnoses of injury in the case of accidents and emergencies, X-rays are vital to ensure the quickest possible care for the accident victim. But X-rays are also used to help diagnose 'non-serious' illness – such as the X-rays often used in a dental surgery. At the moment, there is no alternative to X-rays, but it is thought that they may be dangerous because of the radiation they emit. In the UK, X-rays are thought to contribute to about 1,500 extra cancers every year, of which 750 are fatal.

Until a better technology is found, we are going to have to continue using X-rays, and in many cases the benefits out-weigh the possible risks. But it is a good idea to avoid them unless they are really necessary.

▨ *What can you do?*

When you go to the dentist ask if X-rays are absolutely necessary.

If you have to have an X-ray, wear a lead shield, which blocks the rays entering parts of your body other than the part which needs examination. It is particularly important that you protect your lower abdomen, as the radioactivity in X-rays is thought to affect the reproductive organs.

Don't have X-rays if you think you may be pregnant – it is known that radiation can damage an embryo.

You

It's nearly the end of the book. Over a hundred environmental issues have been presented to you.

From now on, it's up to you. Decide which of the issues are most important to you, find out more about them, join forces with other people if you want to, and take action.

If we were to express all the time the planet has been in existence – 15 billion years – as a 24-hour day, our solar system emerged at about 6 p.m. Life began at around 8 p.m., the dinosaurs walked from 11.35 p.m. to four minutes to midnight, and our ancestors only began walking upright ten seconds ago. The Industrial Revolution and all our modern age have lasted less than a thousandth of a second. During that time, we have ransacked, polluted, bulldozed and bruised the planet so badly that it may not recover. Now we must do something to heal it.

The clock is still ticking. Over to you . . .

Zoos

There are many different types of zoos. Although it is generally thought that zoos which house animals in cages are not as good as areas like national parks and animal parks, where the animals can roam free, all zoos have a role to play in helping preserve some of the world's ENDANGERED SPECIES. With one species becoming extinct every day, zoos are a way of protecting and saving them. They act as a sort of 'Noah's Ark'.

In 1989, a Brazilian giant tarantula gave birth to two hundred tiny baby tarantulas in London Zoo. The press said that this was a miracle because so few giant tarantulas are now left in their native HABITAT. Tarantulas are only one species which is becoming extinct through poaching for private collections. Tigers, monkeys, ELEPHANTS and exotic birds are all captured for the same reasons.

Zoos cannot be the only option for securing any animal's future. It is far better to support nature reserves and the protection of species in wilderness areas.

■ What can you do?

Zoos often face difficulties because of lack of funds to keep them going. If you have a zoo or a nature park near you contact them.

Contact Zoo Check and the Captive Animals Protection Society.

Appendix

Group Action – How to set up and run a group

Setting up your group

Below is a basic checklist for setting up a group – a local group, or one made up of people from your school or college. It should help ensure that things go reasonably smoothly, so your group can take off, run and act.

1. Gather together like-minded friends to help.

2. If you are at school or college, inform the teaching staff. They need to know that you want to set up a group and that you will be having meetings. Some of them may even want to join in.

3. Hold an initial meeting with your like-minded friends. Use this meeting to plan what the first meeting of the full group will be and fix a date that doesn't clash with other events for the first 'official' group meeting.

4. Find a venue – anywhere from the front room at home, if your parents approve, to your local hall, school library or common room. You might need to book in advance.

5. Decide who is going to speak – an invited speaker or someone from within the group?

6. Publicise the meeting. Tell everyone, produce a poster or leaflet with the date, time, place and subject of the meeting clearly marked. Have a look at other posters to get some ideas.

7. Plan an agenda for the first meeting. This should include the time to be allocated to each item and a list of what decisions should be made.

8. On the day, turn up a bit early, with plenty of (recycled) paper. Arrange chairs and organise the refreshments if there are going to be any, so that when people arrive you will be free to greet them.

9. Introduce your speaker, or the video or film, or the subject you will talk about. Try to allow everyone to ask questions if

they want to and discuss things, but try not to let one person dominate.

10. Be realistic. You won't be able to do everything at once. If you want to raise money, decide specifically what you want to raise it for. If people promise to write letters, try to see that they do.

11. Ask someone to make brief notes – 'minutes' – of what happens at the meeting, so that you can refer to them afterwards.

12. Get everyone's name and address, so you know exactly who attended and you can contact them afterwards. Make sure that everyone has been asked to donate whatever is necessary to cover the costs of the meeting – this should obviously be kept to a minimum.

13. Thank everyone for attending before they leave, so that people go away positive. Have fun – meetings aren't supposed to be boring and stuffy. Before you finish, decide what you want to do next. Have another meeting, an action or perhaps even do nothing.

Running your group

Let's assume that the group has now taken off. There are different ways of operating. Some groups prefer not to have people with titles and too many specific labels or tasks, but other groups work better with a treasurer, chair, secretary and other officials. You will have to decide for yourselves how formal you want the group to be.

Whatever happens, some people will have to take responsibility for certain things. Usually these fall into the areas below:

Membership. If you decide to have members, somebody will need to take their details and bank any money you get from membership.

Money. Somebody will need to know how to look after the money and bank it, as well as being able to tell the group how much money they have available at any given time.

Publicity. This person can be responsible for publicising meetings, getting leaflets and posters printed and distributed and even contacting the local press. They could also be responsible for any newsletters, and a small leaflet setting out the aims and ideas of the group, which can be very useful for giving to people who may be interested in joining.

Secretary. This doesn't mean typist! It means someone who can keep tabs on everything that is happening in the group, making sure that all its members are kept in touch with what's going on and that all the administration of the group runs smoothly. The secretary is usually also responsible for keeping minutes (see 11 above) of all meetings. The minutes of the previous meeting are sometimes read to kick off each new meeting thereafter.

It is up to you how you choose these representatives. It is also up to you whether you have one person as a 'chair' or 'administrator' of the group, who has the final decision on things and who is the main spokesperson for the group. You don't have to have an administrator – many groups run as co-operatives, with everyone having a say.

It is important that the people who take these roles – and any others you might want to create – really enjoy doing it. There's no point in doing something you don't want to do. Martyrs rarely win campaigns!

You will also need to set up a contact – a person or a place – that people can approach when they hear about you. Hand them a leaflet explaining who you are and what you do, if you have one. Be inventive, informative and active. You will find that the more positive you are, the more people, help and money will come your way.

Be specific about what you want to do, and don't try to achieve too much at once. Go for one target at first. Watch out for when things go wrong, because that will help you spot potential trouble the next time around.

Sample letters

Dear Council Officer,
(find out the name by telephoning your council office)

I am writing to voice my protest at the proposed new motorway that is to be built in my area. I believe that this motorway will cause major environmental problems. The additional traffic will lead to an increase in accidents and pollution. The new motorway will also cut off the area of my home from my school.

I do not think that your council has considered the views and needs of the whole community. Better public transport in the area would be more efficient and less damaging to the environment. Can you please tell me what you intend to do when the number of cars travelling on this proposed motorway exceeds its capacity? Will you build another and another?

I would be grateful for a reply.

Yours sincerely,

(your name here)

Dear Madam/Sir,

I am writing to you to complain about your hair shampoo. I understand that your company is at present still testing the effects of your shampoo on animals such as rabbits and mice, as you have done for several years. I believe that it is unnecessary and cruel to test a product like yours on animals. Your product has been on the market for some twenty years – surely you know if it is harmful by now!

Could you let me know why you still test your products on animals and when your company will agree to ban such testing? I would be grateful for a reply.

Yours faithfully,

(your name here)

Addresses to contact

Organisations that can help

Voluntary organisations are often short of cash. If you are writing to them for information, please enclose a stamped addressed envelope and give them a clear idea of what you want.

GENERAL INFORMATION AND CAMPAIGNING
GROUPS

Ark Trust
500 Harrow Road, London W9 3QA
Tel 01-968 6780

Campaign for Nuclear Disarmament
22 Underwood Street, London N1
Tel 01-250 4010

Friends of the Earth – Earth Action
26 Underwood Street, London N1 7JQ
Tel 01-490 1555

Greenpeace
30–31 Islington Green, London N1 8BR
Tel 01-354 5100

Intermediate Technology Development Group
103 Southampton Row, London WC1
Tel 01-436 9761

Women's Environmental Network
287 City Road, London EC1V 1LA
Tel 01-490 2511

World Wide Fund for Nature (WWF)
Panda House, Weyside Park, Catteshall Lane, Godalming,
Surrey, GU7 1XR
Tel 04834 26444

ANIMALS

Animal Aid
7 Castle Street, Tonbridge, Kent TN9 1BH

British Union for the Abolition of Vivisection
16a Crane Grove, London N7 8LB

Chicken's Lib
PO Box 2, Holmfirth, Huddersfield, West Yorkshire
HD7 1QT

Compassion in World Farming
20 Lavant Street, Petersfield, Hampshire GU32 3EW

Environmental Investigation Agency
208–209 Upper Street, London N1 IRL

Hunt Saboteurs Association
PO Box 87, Exeter, Devon EX4 3TX

League Against Cruel Sports
Sparling House, 83–87 Union Street, London SE1 1SG

National Anti-Vivisection Society
51 Harley Street, London W1N 1DD

Royal Society for the Protection of Cruelty to Animals
The Causeway, Horsham, West Sussex RH12 1HG

Royal Society for the Protection of Birds
The Lodge, Sandy, Bedfordshire SE1 2DL

Whale and Dolphin Conservation Society
20 West Lea Road, Bath, Avon BA1 3RL

Young People's Trust for Endangered Species
19 Quarry Street, Guildford, Surrey GU1 3EH

Zoo Check
Cherry Tree Cottage, Coldharbour, Dorking, Surrey RH5 6HA

ENERGY

Consumers Against Nuclear Energy
PO Box 697, London NW1 8YQ

Friends of the Earth
26 Underwood Street, London N1 7JQ

Greenpeace
30–31 Islington Green, London N1 8BR

Neighbourhood Energy Action
Energy Projects Office, 2nd Floor, Sunlight Chambers,
2–4 Bigg Market, Newcastle upon Tyne, NE1 1VW

Scram
11 Forth Street, Edinburgh, EH1 3LE

FOOD

London Food Commission
88 Old Street, London EC1V 9AR

Soil Association
86 Colston Street, Bristol BS1 5BB

Vegan Society
33-35 George Street, Oxford, OX1 2AY

The Vegetarian Society
Parkdale, Dunham Road, Altrincham, Cheshire WA14 4QG

HEALTH

Action Against Allergy
43 The Downs, London SW20 8HG

British Holistic Medical Association
179 Gloucester Place, London NW1

Health Education Authority
Hamilton House, Mabledon Place, London WC1H 9TX

Institute for Complementary Medicine
21 Portland Place, London W1N 3AF

HOLIDAYS

British Trust for Conservation Volunteers
36 St Mary's Street, Wallingford, Oxfordshire OX10 OEU

Centre for Alternative Technology
Llwyngwern Quarry, Machynlleth, Powys North Wales

Forest School Camps
110 Burbage Road, London SE24 9HD

Working Weekends on Organic Farms
19 Bradford Road, Lewes, Sussex BN7 1RB

Young Archaeologists Club
United House, Piccadilly, York Y01 1PQ

Youth Hostels Association
Trevelyan House, 8 St Stephen's Hill, St Alban's,
Hertfordshire AL1 2DY

NATURE AND WILDLIFE

Common Ground
45 Shelton Street, London WC2H 9HJ

Countryside Commission
John Dower House, Crescent Place, Cheltenham,
Gloucestershire GL50 3RA

Friends of the Earth Countryside Campaign
26 Underwood Street, London N1 7JQ

Ramblers Association
1–5 Wandsworth Road, London SW8 2XX

Watch Trust for Environmental Education
22 The Green, Nettleham, Lincoln LN2 2NR

World Wide Fund for Nature (WWF)
Panda House, Weyside Park, Catteshall Lane, Godalming,
Surrey GU7 1XR

Young People's Trust for the Environment and Nature
Conservation
95 Woodbridge Rd, Guildford, Surrey, GU1 4PY

POLLUTION

Friends of the Earth
26 Underwood Street, London N1 7JQ

Greenpeace
30–31 Islington Green, London N1 8BR

London Hazards Centre
3rd Floor, Headland House, 308 Grays Inn Road, London
WC1X 8DS

Noise Abatement Society
PO Box 8, Bromley, Kent BR2 OUH

SEAS

Greenpeace
30–31 Islington Green, London N1 8BR

Marine Conservation Society
9 Gloucester Road, Ross-on-Wye, HR9 5BU

Seas at Risk
22 Marks Close, Ingatestone, Essex CM4 9AR

TRAVEL

Campaign for Lead Free Air
3 Endsleigh Street, London WC1H ODD

Community Transport Association
Highbank, Halton Street, Cheshire SK14 2NY

Cyclists Touring Club
69 Meadrow, Godalming, Surrey GU7 3HS

Pedestrians Association
1 Wandsworth Road, London SW8 2LJ

Royal Society for the Prevention of Accidents
Cannon House, The Priory, Queensway, Birmingham,
B4 6BS

Transport 2000
Walkden House, 10 Melton Street, London NW1 2EJ

TREES AND FORESTS

Men of Trees
Crawley Down, Crawley, Sussex RH10 4HL

Woodland Trust
Autumn Park, Dysart Road, Grantham, Lincolnshire
NG31 6LL

TRIBAL PEOPLES

Survival International
310 Edgware Road, London W2 1DY

WASTE

Alucan
Suite 308, 1 Mex House, 52 Blucher St, Birmingham B1 1QU

Can Makers Federation
36 Grosvenor Gardens, London SW1W OED

Friends of the Earth
26 Underwood Street, London N1 7JQ

Industry Council for Packaging and the Environment
Premier House, 10 Greycoat Place, London SW1

London Waste Regulation Authority
Room 174, County Hall, London SE1 7PB

Tidy Britain Group
Premier House, 12 Hatton Garden, London EC1

RESOURCES FOR TEACHERS

Centre for Global Education
University of York, Heslington, York YO1 5DD

Council for Environmental Education
University of Reading, London Road, Reading RG1 5AQ

Green Teacher
Llys Awel, 22 Heol Pentrerhedyn, Machynlleth, Powys, North Wales

National Association of Development Education Centres
6 Endsleigh Street, London WC1H ODX

WWF Teachers Information Service
Panda House, Weyside Park, Catteshall Lane, Godalming, Surrey GU7 1XR

Where to make your views known

MEMBERS OF PARLIAMENT

Get the name of your Member of Parliament from your local council or library. Address them as 'Ms Smith MP' on the envelope and 'Dear Ms Smith' in the letter.

SUPERMARKETS AND COMPANIES

All companies that manufacture products are required to put their address on the packet so you can write to them quite easily. Supermarket headquarters are listed in the phone directory.

Use your library for addresses of other companies and industry, or consult the Citizens Advice Bureau.

Australia and New Zealand

Australian Conservation Foundation
GPO Box 1875, Canberra, ACT 2601

Friends of the Earth
366 Smith Street, Collingwood, Victoria 3066

Friends of the Earth
PO Box 39, 065 Auckland West, New Zealand

Greenpeace New Zealand
Private Bag, Wellesley Street, Auckland,
New Zealand

Illawarra Environmental Centre
Suite 11, 157 Crown Street, Wollongong, NSW 2500

Rainforest Information Centre
PO Box 368, Lismore, NSW 2480

Total Environment Centre
18 Argyle Street, Sydney, NSW 2000

Wilderness Society
130 Davey Street, Hobart, TAS 7000

World Wide Fund for Nature
Box 6237, Wellington, New Zealand

Canada

Friends of the Earth/Les Amis de la Terre
251 Laurier Avenue West, Suite 701, Ottawa, Ontario
KIP 5J6

World Wide Fund for Nature
201 St Clair Avenue East, Toronto, Ontario, M4T 1NS

Ecology Action Centre
1657 Barrington Street, Suite 520, Halifax, Nova Scotia,
B3J 2A1

Greenpeace
427 Bloor Street West, Toronto, Ontario, M5S 1X7

United States

Earth Island Institute
300 Broadway, Suite 28, San Francisco, CA 94133

Environmental Defense Fund
1616 P Street NW, Suite 150, Washington, DC 20036

Food First
1885 Mission Street, San Francisco, CA 94103

Friends of the Trees
PO Box 1466, Chelan, WA 98816

Global Tomorrow Coalition
1325 G Street NW, Suite 1003, Washington, DC 20005

Greenpeace
1611 Connecticut Ave NW, Washington, DC 20009

Intermediate Technology Group
777 United Nations Development Plaza, New York, NY 10017

Sierra Club
330 Pennsylvania Avenue NW, Washington, DC 20005

Survival International
2121 Decatur Place, Washington, DC 20008

World Resources Institute and Friends of the Earth
218 D Street SE, Washington, DC 20003

Worldwatch Institute
1776 New York Avenue NW, Suite 230, Washington, DC 20036

World Wide Fund for Nature
1250 24th Street NW, Washington, DC 20037

Further reading

The Battle for the Planet, Andre Singer. Pan Books, London 1987

Blueprint for a Green Planet, John Seymour & Herbert Girardet. Dorling Kindersley Ltd, London, 1989

C for Chemicals: Chemical Hazards and How to Avoid Them, Michael Birkin and John Price, Green Print/The Merlin Press Ltd, 1989

Chemical Children: How to Protect your Family from Harmful Pollutants, Peter Mansfield and Jean Monro. Century Hutchinson/David and Charles, London 1988

The Cruelty Free Shopper, Liz Howlett. Available from The Vegan Society Ltd, 33–35 George Street, Oxford OX1 2AY

The New E for Additives, Maurice Hanssen with Jill Marsden. Thorsons Publishing Group, 1987

Ecology For Beginners, Stephen Croall. Pantheon Books, 1981

Energy Without End, Michael Flood. Available from Friends of the Earth, 26–28 Underwood Street, London N1 7QJ

The Friends of the Earth Handbook, ed. Jonathon Porritt. Macdonald Optima, 1986

The Gaia Atlas of Planet Management, ed. Norman Myers. Pan Books, London 1985

The Green Consumer Guide, John Elkington and Julia Hailes. Victor Gollancz Ltd, 1988

Home Ecology, Karen Christensen. Arlington Books, 1989

How To Be Green, John Button. Century, London, 1989

Richard's Bicycle Book, Richard Ballantine. Ballantine Books, 1982

If you would like to be on the Virago Upstart mailing list send
a S.A.E. to:

Virago Upstarts
Virago Press
20-23 Mandela St
Camden Town
London NW1 0HQ